Schooled

Schooled

THE STORY OF AN EDUCATION

• • •

Dr. Lodge McCammon

ISBN: 1983574589
ISBN 13: 9781983574580
Library of Congress Control Number: 2018900485
CreateSpace Independent Publishing Platform
North Charleston, South Carolina

For my parents, Marianela and Gavin, who make all things possible.

Special thanks to these beautiful humans for helping me shape this story:

Dr. Brandy Parker
Michelle Eggleston
Kyle Schutt
Dr. Steven Toaddy
Nick Parker
Robert Maser
Dr. Elizabeth Speights
Lance Bledsoe
Dr. Dave Frye

Contents

Before We Begin

• • •

OVER THE PAST 15 YEARS, I have had the opportunity to be a student, teacher, trainer, speaker, musician, and YouTube creator. I have been incredibly fortunate to work with many school districts, nonprofits, and businesses across the country with the goal of inspiring change in all types of learning environments – from kindergarten classrooms to corporate training sessions. I have spent over a decade researching, writing, presenting, recording, and sharing new ideas with educators and trainers around the world. All that effort has resulted in the creation of something incredibly simple and powerful. I have identified, tested, and continue to use a series of practical research-based instructional strategies that, when implemented together, I call "The McCammon Method" of teaching.[1] I believe this method can be used to enhance many learning environments and I am excited to share the story of its development with you.

The original working title for this book was "The Worst Book About Education Ever Written." Some of my stories and observations are critical of what happens in many classrooms and I was nervous that readers might take offense. I thought that if I called the book "the worst" up front, then nobody could blame me if they were put-off by my suggestions for improving education. After a number of iterations, I felt more secure about

---

1   The McCammon Method Research. Retrieved from
http://schooled.lodgemccammon.com
The website above contains a list of footnotes. I encourage you to explore each link in sequence as you progress through the story.

what I was sharing and decided to change the title to "Schooled: The Story of an Education," because it better represents what you are about to read. It's my story. The good. The bad. The weird. The critical.

Though I am not a writer by trade, I do enjoy the challenge of weaving together ideas using the written word. This means that much of the text might seem somewhat diary-like, informal, and many times silly. My writing style is simply the pragmatic result of trying to deliver my thoughts as honestly as possible. I have also included footnotes throughout the book, many of which provide links to resources that help illustrate my story. I sincerely hope you find this book to be an easy and enjoyable read.

One last thing, and then I will stop all the caveats. It's likely that as you're diving into my story you may think, "Good grief, this guy is extremely privileged and sometimes even arrogant!" As you will come to find out, I have been handed many incredible opportunities, several of which were crucial in enabling me to develop as a professional. I recognize and appreciate my good fortune; thus, I have tried to give back more than I have received. So, if you ever feel yourself thinking poorly of me, please remember that my main motivation, like so many other educators, is to make the world a better place.

Let's begin the story of an education.

CHAPTER 1

Childhood

• • •

I GREW UP THE SON of Gavin and Marianela McCammon in Barrington, Illinois, a northwest suburb of Chicago. I lived there from birth until 18 years old when I left for college. I had what I consider to be a fairly typical schooling experience. From kindergarten through 12th grade, I attended the public school that my district provided, and I was an average student. And throughout those years, I had a few memorable teachers.

My childhood home in Barrington, Illinois.

My fifth grade teacher, Mrs. Thornhill, stands out. She developed a classroom economy. Students rented desks until they could own them. We received "Scholar Dollars" as payment for excelling academically and behaviorally. We were required to start a company and sell a good or service (i.e., desk cleaning, lottery, friendship bracelets). This was the first time I realized that the lottery was a regressive tax, a heavier burden on those with less wealth.

Allow me to recall and reteach this lesson from when I was 11 years old. The money that less wealthy individuals spend on the lottery accounts for a larger percentage of their income. As it turns out, students who were the poorest (in the Scholar Dollar sense, not spiritually) were the most likely to let it ride on the lottery, ultimately spending the most. This also tends to happen in real life. Lower income can mean less education and less education means that one might not understand the chances of winning the lottery – which are miniscule. Even if the poorer students were to spend the same amount as wealthier students, it would still have a larger impact on them. A regressive tax means that the less wealthy pay a higher percentage of their salaries by spending the same amount of money as the more wealthy. For example, if you make $10 per day and spend $1 on the lottery, then you are spending 10 percent of your income on the lottery. However, if you make $20 per day and spend $1 on the lottery, you are only spending 5 percent of your income. That's a regressive tax. Pretty cool economic lesson to learn as a fifth grader, right?

I also learned that the lottery could be an extremely lucrative venture. My friend Gavin, the owner and operator of the classroom lottery, cleaned up financially. I honestly don't recall what my business was, but I did all right and was mainly interested in spending every Scholar Dollar I could muster to purchase other students' desks, so I could collect rent. I was also very interested in Fridays because that was auction day. We were allowed to bring in goodies from home (e.g., candy, cookies, etc.) to auction off. A large package of Sour Patch Kids sold for a pretty (Scholar) penny.

The virtual field trips were also super radical. A few times each semester we would be allowed to "take a flight" to see a faraway land. For example, during the fall we visited France. Mrs. Thornhill set up a projector and screen in order to show a film about the history of Paris. The amount of Scholar Dollars we were willing to spend on the trip determined if we sat in first class or coach. We set up our chairs in rows like an airplane, with first class closest to the screen and coach farthest away. First class was served grape juice and cookies while those sitting in coach were served water and peanuts. I saved my money and sat in coach. First class seemed pretentious and frivolous given my tight budget.

Halfway through the year we were assigned to complete a science project. I had been playing music most of my life up to this point, so I decided to do something with acoustics. My grandfather helped me with my project by getting ahold of two refrigerator boxes. We lined one with carpet padding and the other with tin foil. We cut out a hole in each big enough for someone to stick his or her head inside. I put a speaker in each box that played music, so people would stick their head in and describe the difference between the two sounds. While I don't recall the details of the results, I do remember thinking it was pretty cool that I got to play my Def Leppard tapes (yes, tapes) during the fifth grade science fair. Through these activities and countless others, Mrs. Thornhill created an exciting and active learning environment.

My entire school experience at North Barrington Elementary was pretty rad. I liked going to school. I was a decent student, not nearly the top of the class or fully dedicated to the task of learning, but I did what needed to be done. I was good at following rules, standing quietly in line, sitting quietly and staying under the radar. I also produced a respectable amount of enthusiasm when given a chance to do an activity beyond the "sit and learn" standard that started around third or fourth grade.

Then came Barrington Middle School. Oh, the horror! It was like a switch was flipped. I don't want to be hyperbolic, but yuck. Starting in seventh grade, every day felt virtually the same. It was like I started middle school and someone said, "OK, you are not kids anymore, so no more fun stuff. Sit there and listen. Write things down. Take this test. Go to your next class. Repeat." With a few exceptions, that was the general lesson plan in my middle school, high school, college, master's, and Ph.D. classes. That's almost 20 years of sit the heck down, shut the front door and listen up because this is going to be on the dang test!

During the first few weeks of middle school, I longed for my elementary classrooms and teachers. But thinking about it now, the biggest difference was that in elementary school we did more projects and moved through the content at a slower pace. And upon further contemplation, the schooling part was not much different. Since I can remember, even back in elementary school, most of the classroom time was spent on the teacher delivering information to us, the students, and our passive acceptance, or in some cases, an active resistance of said information. It's just that as I got older, I became numb to this schooling process. As there became more and more distance from Scholar Dollars and science fairs, I began to accept what school was going to be from now on: dull and boring. Soon after this acceptance, I joined the ranks of most kids in agreeing, in concert, that "school stinks" because it did. Figuratively and sometimes literally.

Barrington High School was similarly numbing with few exceptions. One of those exceptions was a teacher named Mr. Mott who I had as a sophomore. He taught Contemporary World Affairs, which was an elective. He was essentially a standup comedian and breathed excitement into the prison that was Barrington High School. Every day I would shuffle (in the coolest possible way) to his third-period classroom to laugh for 47 minutes and learn about what was going on in the world, and discover why we should care. Think of John Stewart from Comedy Central's Daily Show as a high school teacher. That was Mr. Mott.

The other exception was the economics class I took my senior year. Sadly, I can't seem to recall the teacher's name, but honestly it was not the teacher that made the difference for me. The class was extremely typical. It followed the same mundane pattern of learning that I had experienced since seventh grade. I sat in a chair and listened to lectures. Then I did some worksheets and bookwork to kill what was left of class time. However, this was the first time that I really enjoyed a subject. Economics was my jam!

Looking back on this public schooling, I am faced with a conundrum. From kindergarten all the way through high school, I spent most of the time sitting and listening to information being delivered by teachers, with few exceptions. The problem is that I turned out pretty well. I am an intelligent guy who has made what I believe to be a significant (and growing) contribution to an industry. How could this be? Half of these years I did not really like school. And even during the years I did enjoy it, I never really pushed myself to excel. I was decidedly average. My schooling never really challenged me, it allowed me to be average, but had a good outcome. Is it fair to judge school harshly? Is it fair to criticize and demand that the industry change? Maybe, but let's come back to that in just a second after this side note.

Side note: Even though I might be pleased with the way I turned out, I have to believe that maybe it's in spite of my schooling. There is compelling research that suggests parents have a much bigger impact on the success of a student than schools and teachers. I am beyond lucky that my parents are wonderful. So, I suppose it's easier for me to attribute my success to them than to my teachers. Parenting is critical and there are many books and resources about that topic. However, let's keep our focus on what happens and can happen in classrooms.

Many in the education industry seem to value having active learning environments for all students. Why? Well, it's really easy to disengage in the classroom when you are not actively involved in the education process. We know from research that if we can engage students actively in the learning (e.g., working in groups, asking questions, peer teaching, creating artifacts of learning, etc.), it can increase success.[2]

A Kid in College

It seemed the further I got in school, the worse the issue became, and the more inactive my learning became. At Maryville College (where I completed my bachelor's degree from 1996-1999), the amount of "sit there and take in information from an instructor" was very close to 100 percent of the time. The difference was that now I was paying lots of money for this passive learning experience. The more I paid, the more lecture I got. I suppose the idea was that in college and university one pays for knowledge from those who hold the knowledge. Professors hold the knowledge, and I pay per credit hour to have the privilege of hearing that information. Though, I honestly didn't think much of it back then. I just assumed that this was how school worked. I had seen the same thing for many years and I was moderately successful in this model of learning. I adapted, like most of us did. I learned how to pretend to pay attention. I learned when I needed to listen and when I could space out. I learned which professors could be completely tuned out because the test was only going to cover the information in the textbook.

One statistics professor started the first day of class by saying, "You are all adults and professional learners. Therefore, you should be able to listen to my lectures, take notes, read the text, and study hard to be successful in this class." At the time, I remember thinking that he was justifying the fact that the class was going to be super boring and filled with lecture. It was, on both accounts.

---

2 Active learning increases student performance in science, engineering, and mathematics. Retrieved from http://schooled.lodgemccammon.com

Similar to my K-12 public school experience, there were moments in college that stood out. For example, we were required to write a senior thesis, a light version of a master's thesis, except we were not required to conduct a study. It was mainly a review of the literature on a particular topic.

I was majoring in economics, so I decided to write about how the Department of Justice's merger guidelines impacted the banking industry. Exciting, right? This was a big deal back in the mid-90s and I enjoyed researching this topic and writing the thesis.

I also preferred classes when the professors had interesting personalities. In particular, Dr. Maren had this brilliant air about him as he lectured on philosophy of religion. Dr. Bob's lectures on international trade and finance were detailed and funny because of his excitement for the subject matter. Dr. Prince's human health and development lectures were very entertaining. And Dr. Kramer's lectures were awesome because they were about economics. Regardless of the amount of content I mastered in these classes, I enjoyed the personalities of these professors and took a little something from each of them, integrating it into the way I communicate with people to this day.

It's my understanding that my college experience, based upon discussions with others, was fairly typical. Academically, college was literally (figuratively) filled with a metric ton of sitting and listening to lecture. Thus, I got better and better at pretending to listen attentively as the years went by. I figured that being a professional student meant having the ability to sit for hours and persevere through extreme inactivity and boredom. Now, keep in mind, this was before students even had cell phones and computers with them in class. Back then, I would pretend to pay attention by allowing my mind to wander, pondering things like what color Jell-O would be in the cafeteria for lunch or where the party would be this weekend. You know, the important stuff.

CHAPTER 2

After College, Between Tennis and Soup

• • •

I GRADUATED FROM MARYVILLE COLLEGE in the summer of 1999 with a degree in economics. My parents came down to Tennessee from Barrington for the graduation ceremony. Actually, they were attending both my graduation from Maryville College and my sister's graduation from the University of Tennessee School of Law. I pulled my dad aside and said, "Hey pop, I just graduated with a degree in economics, what should I do now?" He responded by saying, "If you don't know what to do, go to law school."

I didn't have much experience with lawyers up to this point in my life. I was generally a rule-follower. I had done exactly zero underage drinking, nor had I experimented with any illegal substances. Although some of my comrades had been busted for this or that over the years and required the services of a lawyer, I required nothing. It seemed that my existence enjoyed the avoidance of being hassled. Plus, I had heard lots of lawyer jokes since my sister was now qualified to be one, and it did not exactly encourage me to jump head first in that direction. My favorite was "What do you call 5,000 dead lawyers at the bottom of the ocean? A good start." Now, I know this is technically a riddle, not a joke, but you get the idea.

The thought of law school was deplorable for many reasons, including the fact that I didn't consider myself a "good student" and law school would be super difficult and academically demanding. Thus, I responded to my dad by saying, "Uh, I don't want to go to law school" to which he replied, "Well, then do whatever you want to do." To be clear, he didn't say this in a snarky tone, but in a supportive way. Soon after that conversation, I packed up my Dodge Stealth and moved to North Hollywood.

On a bench in LA

I moved to LA to attend a recording school. I had been playing and recording music most of my life and wanted to learn more about the engineering side of music production. I attended a few weeks of this school and was quite dismayed by the teaching methods. This was a training program about audio engineering and the first two weeks of class consisted of sitting in a room listening to lectures. There was no evidence that these teaching methods were going to drastically change at any point during the course, so I politely excused myself, hung around California for a short while longer, and then headed back east. As I drove from LA to Chicago, I thought, among many other things, how strange it was for an audio engineering program to be so heavily reliant on lecture. I figured it would be largely hands-on. These passive learning experiences had been the norm for many years, but I was still disappointed that they had not made the learning experience more active and exciting.

After my time in LA, and a short visit to my childhood home in the suburbs of Chicago, I moved to Nashville, Tennessee. I lived in an apartment in Brentwood with three other dudes. One of them, Chris, was a friend I made at Maryville College. We had recorded and played a little music together while in my dorm room. After he graduated (two years before me), he moved out to Nashville to pursue a career in country music.

At the end of 1999, I assembled a portable 32-track digital recording studio. I packed this studio into a case that resembled a coffin and would travel to venues or practice spaces around Nashville and record musicians and bands. It was interesting work.

After a few months, I decided that Nashville was not for me, so I moved back to Maryville, Tennessee and lived in a shed behind my sister and brother-in-law's house. They were recently married, and I recall telling them that I would be living in the shed "just for a few months until I figure out what I want to do next." They were so gracious and allowed me to hang around. You might be wondering if the shed had running water. Nope. You also might be wondering how big this shed was. Maybe 300 square feet. It had no central heat or air, but I did have a window AC unit and some space heaters.

The Shed

A few months turned into three and a half years.

The first two years (1999-2001) were filled with listlessness, jobless-ness, exercise, tennis, and frequent lunches at a place called the Soup Kitchen with a small number of college friends who were still in town. It was an odd existence. I literally had an extended period of time where I had absolutely zero accountability for being.

The biggest downside, beyond living in a shed, was that my parents were forced to answer questions about me from friends, family, and ac-quaintances. People would ask questions like "How is Lodge?" My parents would have to respond by saying things like, "Oh, he's still living in the shed behind our daughter's house, trying to figure things out."

Not one time during those years in the shed did my parents make me feel bad for the choices I had made. They would say things to me like, "You'll figure it out" and "You'll find something to be passionate about." Yup, I have the best parents on the planet. Who else would allow, enable, and even encourage such shenanigans? Nobody. I am fortunate, and they were absolutely right that I would figure something out, but it took two years.

After two years of shed life, I needed a change. It was time to figure out a way to use my economic reasoning to contribute to society. To that end, I called my dad and said, "I have been living in this shed for two years and I'm not sure what I should do." He replied, "If you don't know what to do, go to law school." Really, again? After a long and heavy breath, I said "OK. Great idea." It was something to do, and I desperately needed something to do. Between you, me, and the thin aluminum walls of that little shed, I was going a little insane. I spent an inordinate amount of time by myself and I had grown numb to the influx of different critters. I had been confronted with bats, opossums, crickets and ants on the regular. It was when I started to think of them as pets rather than pests that I knew I was desperate enough to attempt law school.

Sometimes I hear people say that they wished for unlimited free time, so they could do nothing. Not many people are ever afforded that opportunity, especially in their early to mid-20s. And to refresh, we are not talking about unlimited time in addition to unlimited resources. We are talking about unlimited time living in a shed in rural Tennessee. Yes, for the first few months it was totally great. I filled my time with music and projects. But then, it became harder to think of new songs and projects. So, I started reading a lot. After a few months of that, it grew old. Soon, it turned into just trying to do anything to pass the time. And that is where I had been for quite a while. Frankly, just killing time is no way to live. Life is short. Each day is an opportunity where every minute matters, and I was ready to start taking advantage of my life.

Since I did have unlimited free time, I allocated some of it to researching what it took to get into law school. Now, as a reminder, the shed was behind my sister's house and she had graduated from law school. When I told her that I was interested in attending law school, she said two words that, at the time didn't really sway me much: "It's awful." Despite her input, I was going to do it anyway.

LSAT

To get into law school, I discovered that I needed a college degree in pretty much anything. I had one in economics. Check. I also needed to take a test called the Law School Admission Test (LSAT). Then, I would send my transcripts and test score along with an application to a school that has a law program. After receiving those materials, they would let me know if I was good enough to attend their school. If so, they would let me come to their campus to learn the law. After two years of being in the shed, that seemed like a rather tenable process and a challenge. In other words, I finally had something to do.

I purchased a large LSAT preparation book from the local bookstore. Every day I spent three hours, scheduled around my tennis playing and soup eating, working on practice problems to familiarize myself with the test format. The book said that it was one of the most important aspects of test preparation. The idea was that if you're used to the test format, you won't be surprised when it counts. I did this for a month and then I signed up for the LSAT.

The test was administered on the University of Tennessee campus. It was in a classroom that had stadium seating and every other seat was filled with an eager future lawyer. Immediately, I was reminded of that joke (riddle). "What do you call 5,000 lawyers at the bottom of the ocean?" I giggled to myself as I got situated in my chair and arranged my pencils on the table in front of me. They handed out the test and read the directions aloud. I already knew the drill because I went through the LSAT preparation book. The LSAT administrator said, "begin" and out of nowhere, I panicked. I was not able to focus on the series of logic problems. I started skimming the text and guessing wildly, hoping that luck would prevail. The test ended, and I drove home numb. Now I had to wait a few weeks to find out how I did.

The LSAT company offered a service where I could pay $5 to find out my score before it was mailed to me. All I had to do was call a phone number, enter a credit card number and an automated voice would tell me the score. I vividly remember calling that darn number, entering my information and waiting in silence, for what seemed like a full minute, to hear my score. I am sure it was only three seconds. But the number that I heard was essentially a failing grade. The number was significantly lower than the LSAT requirement for any school I was considering. Thus, with the push of a button, I heard that, quite frankly, I was not qualified to attend law school. By the way, I'm still insecure about my score, so I am not going to tell you what it was.

That hit me like a ton of bricks. I had never really failed at anything before. I had never been told that I was not smart enough to do something that I wanted to do. It was a major bummer. I sustained a significant scream-cry session on the floor of that little shed and was filled with ridiculous and sustained self-pity. Then, I got over it and started wondering why I bombed so epically.

Test anxiety is real, and nasty, and real nasty. Apparently, living in a shed for two years does not do an excellent job at preparing one to take an intimidating test like the LSAT. While my acquaintances, the aforementioned critters (bats and such), would whisper encouraging words while I slept, it turned out that they were not very helpful when it came to being successful on standardized tests. I was living an extremely non-standardized life and apparently my mind had a hard time adjusting to that room with those pencils and questions.

In addition, I carried a lot of anticipation into that test. The test was my way out of the shed. The test was my way of redeeming myself to my family. The test was my (dad's) purpose. I epically failed in part because I carried all of that into the room with me. I sat down in that chair and had a full-on panic attack while I was trying to figure out if A can be next to C and D but can't be adjacent to E or F while G is across from both H and I. That's what those questions seemed like to me. The LSAT is filled with a bunch of logic-reasoning questions that are difficult to understand, let alone answer.

I know that test anxiety is real because I took the LSAT again. Oh, you thought I was going to just quit and continue to hide in the shed? No way. I was unable to simply absorb that level of failure without a measured response. In this case, the response was to take the test again and do better. I did. This time I did not study, and I did not carry all that anticipation into the room with me. I got a much better (respectable) score, though still rather low, but good enough to get into the school I was interested in attending.

Two months later, I received an email from the law school of my choice saying that I had been accepted. I rejoiced and celebrated the day with an extra bowl of soup. I called people and bragged. Now, there was no Facebook in 2002, but this news would have received at least 150 likes and 75 comments. Most of those comments would surely be of the generic variety exclaiming "Congratulations" (or "Congrats" if the acquaintance was trying to save a little time). I felt relief. I had a purpose. My parents were happy. My sister just shook her head. Everything was on track.

That night I could not fall asleep. It was not because I was excited about my new upcoming journey. I was haunted by the crystal-clear, laser-focused thought that I had absolutely no interest in going to law school. I was troubled by the fact that I was going to be taking a seat at a school, not allowing someone else the opportunity to learn about the law who was actually excited about it and wanted to be there. I was concerned that I would be spending the next three years sitting in classrooms listening to lectures about and discussing case law.

A few hours into this thought process, at two in the morning, I called my dad. He is usually awake at all hours. He answered the phone and I simply said, "I don't want to go to law school" and he replied, "That's OK. Just do whatever you want to do." Again, he didn't say it sarcastically or with any type of judgment. He said it sincerely. Amazing parents, right? I am the luckiest son-of-a-person ever, but while relieved that I would not be attending law school, I was back at square one. I had no idea what I wanted to do.

One of my closest friends at the time was a kindergarten teacher at a nearby school. I decided to carve out some time between tennis and soup to visit her school and volunteer. Specifically, I would sit with kids one-on-one during centers (when students are in groups rotating between activities) and work with them on phonics. Saying that I was working with them is hyperbole. I would sit and encourage kids as they read simple words, painstakingly sounding them out.

When the students would fumble, I would help. When they would mispronounce, I would correct. When they would get it right, I would encourage. When students would accidently slip in a cuss word, I would look around hoping that nobody else heard it. They did not say the F-word on purpose, and most of the time they didn't know they had said it. I am sure it's something they heard on the playground or at home. It got stuck in their little five-year-old brain and it came tumbling out during Mr. Lodge time. Lucky me.

After each tutoring session, I would hand the student a sticker, make a funny face and say something like, "Solid reading, you super sandwich." They would laugh. I would laugh and then tell them to "shove off" or "go away." Again, they would crack up. Working with kids was pretty cool. Teaching. It was an interesting idea. Maybe I'll try that.

CHAPTER 3

Those Who Can't Do

• • •

I HAD NO IDEA HOW I was going to justify my decision to teach. Honestly, I had not been very good at anything, including school. I had been listless and unsure about what to do with my life. I was not really qualified to do much. But I was at the end of my rope and needed to move forward to get out of the shed. It could be argued that I didn't know what else to do, so I decided to teach. I should tell you now that teaching seemed like it would be an easy choice. Teaching does not pay much, so not much would be expected, or so I thought.

Volunteering in that kindergarten classroom did help me determine one justifiable reason for teaching. My parents are such amazing people and I always pictured myself as a parent. I always thought that I would strive to be the best dad imaginable, like the one I had. I told myself that it was OK to go into teaching because it would train me how to raise excellent children. I would learn about how to manage and direct the learning of a child. After all, the point of life, the biological imperative, tells us to have children to pass on both genes and knowledge.

Honestly, I decided to become a teacher for a lot of the wrong reasons and some of the right ones. However, I think quite a few people decided to become teachers for a mixture of these same reasons, and I am certainly not saying that's bad. I'm just saying that it's the way I was feeling at the time. Heading into the industry feeling this way was important given the trajectory of my career. So, keep in mind as you continue to read that I basically decided to be a teacher because I had hit bottom and was trying to find a lifeline.

Teaching, Really?

After I reconciled with the stigma of becoming a teacher (you know, the whole those who can't do thing), my first order of business was to have exhausting and lengthy conversations with every educator I knew about what it's like, what the problems are, what solutions exist, and how it has changed since I was a kid. I greatly enjoyed going into classrooms to observe. Being in a classroom to observe education happening is an entirely different experience than being a student, where education is happening to you. I found myself sitting in the back of many different classrooms furiously taking notes about the dynamics of teaching and learning. I paid attention to what factors made classrooms "feel good" and what made them "feel bad." During most of my observations, I saw exactly what I experienced as a student. Most of the time was spent on lecture while the students were sitting in chairs. Classroom observation became a cornerstone for my future work. I found that it was important to see lots of different classroom environments in order to design methods for improving education at the macro level, pondering trends across thousands of classrooms, not just what happens in one.

I also immediately started spending time on ideas that I considered to be innovative. My mind was engaged in thinking through ways of improving the teaching and learning experience, not just replicating it. Frankly, as I stated before, school kind of stinks and I felt it was my duty as a future teacher to figure out ways of making it not stink, more figuratively than literally. I figured that the actual smells in the hallways and classrooms were janitorial issues, not instructional ones.

I continued thinking deeply about education, focusing on my experiences with it as a student and my ideas on how to change it. I re-enrolled at Maryville College to take the necessary education classes to become eligible for teacher licensure. Since I already had my undergraduate degree, I also applied to an advanced degree program through the University of Tennessee, where I would eventually earn a Master's of Science of Education with a focus in Instructional Technology. All of this happened very quickly during the spring of 2002. I put all my energy toward this new goal.

When my friends found out that I was going back to school to become a teacher, most of them responded by saying something like "Haha! Wait. You're serious? *You* are going to *teach?*" When I would inquire as to why they were indignant about this, their reply was both fascinating and disturbing. Many of them would say something like, "It's strange that you want to teach. You are intelligent and capable. Teaching seems like the wrong fit for someone like you." Obviously, they had not seen my LSAT scores. In response, I told them that I wanted to teach so I could learn how to be a great father someday. There was no way that anyone could judge me for wanting that. The idea was beyond reproach, and I hid behind it so I would not be harshly judged for my decision.

It's important to note here that my friends were not wrong to be slightly indignant. Let's remember the context in which I made this decision. I had just experienced the most aggressive academic failure of my life, performing very poorly on the LSAT. Now, it all turned out OK in the end, and actually resulted in me rejecting the law school acceptance anyway, but my mental state heading into the teaching profession cannot be ignored. Many of my friends questioned whether it was the correct choice based on their opinion that I was "too smart to spend my time in the classroom," especially a public high school classroom.

Generally, the teaching profession does not pull candidates from the top of the college and university talent pool, though the profession does attract some of the most caring people on the planet. My friends were possibly justified in suggesting that it might not be a good fit for me. I graduated in the top 25 percent of my class and I was not known for my warm and caring personality (typical demeanor for economists). Also, around 75 percent of the teaching workforce consisted of women. Maybe there was some cognitive dissonance around that as well, leading my friends to view teaching as something more appropriate for females. Finally, the old chestnut "those who can't do, teach." The possible origin of this statement dates back to a George Bernard Shaw play in 1903, "Man and Superman," where a character exclaimed, "He who can, does; he who cannot, teaches." As much as I dislike that sentiment, it strangely fit in my case.

Self-Righteous Approach

I jumped passionately into my education programs with certain attitudes and expectations. I did not show up on the first day of class excited to learn about a whole new world of education strategies, policy issues, and research. Frankly, I didn't really think that professors had much to teach me. I looked at my education classes as the typical hurdles that needed to be navigated in order to have the privilege of teaching in a public school classroom. Also, my opinion of many teachers was quite low. I felt like most of the teachers I had throughout my schooling did not do much to further my love of learning. In fact, most of them spent the majority of class time lecturing to students who were sitting down. Whatever class time was left was typically filled with assessments and independent or group work. I was quite indignant, negative and somewhat hostile about having to take classes to learn how to lecture. It seemed unnecessary since I had my own ideas about how to improve education.

At 25 years old, I was older than most in my licensure program at Maryville College. Most of the other students were juniors or seniors in college. However, in my graduate classes at the University of Tennessee,

I was one of the youngest. Those classes were filled with current teachers who were going back to school, many who openly admitted that they were doing it for the bump in pay. Many school districts across the country increase pay if a teacher has a master's degree.

At both institutions, I approached these education classes with impassioned self-righteous indignation. I thought I had it figured out. I had been a student in school for 16 years. I had volunteered in kindergarten for a short while. I had put in a little time and energy thinking deeply about teaching and learning. I had postulated theories about why I disliked school so much and had designed some strategies that would make education better for my students. Do you see a serious problem with that state of mind during training? Me too. But why was I acting like this?

It was all about insecurity. Similar to why many of us refuse to admit that our parents might be anything less than ideal, if we admit that our education was cruddy, then we are, in a way, admitting that we are flawed. Screaming at the top of my lungs that I am not flawed is not only the best indication of being flawed, but it's a classic symptom of insecurity. This insecurity encourages us to hide who we really are while defending our personal experience as the gold standard of existence.

One defensive strategy is to focus on the few great teachers we had. Those are the stories we tell when talking about the merits of our educational upbringing. Mrs. Thornhill and Mr. Mott are the pillars of my educational experience. They are the best teachers. In fact, they must be because I turned out great.

While this is arguably a delusional way to navigate the world, it has an interesting impact on many of us who decide to become teachers. Many of us want to be part of the education system so that we can inspire a new generation of citizens. Such a lofty goal requires a certain level of delusion; to think that we are worthy or qualified for that job is quite ambitious.

Again, we have to believe that our education was worthy and excellent because we are worthy and excellent. We cite the exceptions, our best teachers, as the reasons why we are worthy and excellent. Thus, we strive to model our teaching after what worked so well for us, or for what we delude ourselves into believing worked so well.

Here's another way of looking at it. Almost everyone I know will say that they thought school stunk when they were there. With the next breath, they will say that it worked well for them, despite it stinking. Human nature is a very funny thing.

This method of thinking does not leave much wiggle room for being open to new ideas. I walked into my first education classes convinced I had it all figured out. The solution to cruddy education was that we needed more teachers like Mrs. Thornhill and Mr. Mott. My solution was simple. I was going to *be* like them. I was going to express the parts of their personalities that made me enjoy their classrooms. I was going to be successful in the same ways they were. And here is the tricky part that really showed my glaring insecurities – I believed that any other teacher who was not on the same path as me was doing it wrong. That went for my peers in these education programs as well as the professors.

I decided that the solution to the problem of education was that we needed more teachers who have the right temperament and personality that inspire students to want to learn. That had to be the answer because that's what I believe worked for me. Therefore, I approached learning in these classes with that running in the forefront of my mind. It's really difficult to function in classes if that is your mindset. It's like every idea presented outside your belief system is a point of contention. At best, I would have to say that I was closed-minded.

At this point you might be thinking, "Hey buddy, I'm not closed-minded. I love learning. I am always open to learning about new methods and am constantly seeking out critical feedback on who I am and what I do." If you truly are like that then keep reading because you are exceptional, and the rest of this book will hopefully help you understand a little more about the rest of us.

As it happens, hundreds of teachers I have talked to have stories similar to mine. The difference is that their solution to education was based on the personality of *their* favorite teachers, and they thought *I* was doing it wrong because I was emulating the wrong superheroes. Their favorite teachers were not exactly like my favorite teachers. Can you see how this is problematic if we are truly searching for actual solutions to actual problems in education? Can you see how this is problematic if we are trying to develop some type of professional/national standard for teachers? Everyone is convinced they have the answers, and all the answers are different. #Frustrating, right?

This arrogance and self-righteousness got me into a significant amount of trouble in my licensure program. I think everyone pretty much disliked me (peers and professors alike). I approached most assignments as if I knew better. I knew better than the research, texts, articles, other students in the classes, and my professors. I was aggressive with my points of view in all my classes.

A few months into the program at Maryville College, we had to do interviews with the faculty where they would ask questions and give feedback about how we were progressing. I was spouting my normal off-center responses to their questions, railing against standardized tests and sitting in rows, and sharing my thoughts on behavior management and how to inspire a love of learning by being "real" with students. Toward the end, the department head paused and said, "You are going to struggle in public schools because you don't seem to want to follow the rules." I thought about that for a moment and retorted, "The rules have been used to develop a lame education system. The rules are not good enough."

CHAPTER 4
Student Teaching

• • •

THIS ARROGANCE BECAME MORE OF a problem during and after student teaching. In the spring of 2003, since I was pursuing a licensure to teach middle or high school social studies classes, I was to spend three weeks observing and teaching in a middle school social studies classroom. After I completed that, I would spend 10 weeks doing the same in a high school social studies classroom. I was placed at Maryville Middle School and Maryville High School, respectively.

While my interest was in teaching high school, I diligently attended to my middle school placement. I was paired with a younger male teacher named Mr. P. He had excellent control over the kids from a classroom management perspective. The desks were in straight, tight rows. He ran a strict and seemingly efficient learning environment, telling me many times, without any semblance of compunction, that the focus of his work with the kids was on increasing test scores. Thus, his teaching was extremely formulaic. In each period, the students would come in and immediately complete an assessment (many times a short multiple choice quiz) on previous knowledge. That assessment would be briefly discussed and student questions would be answered. Then Mr. P would spend 20 to 30 minutes lecturing to cover new information. The balance of the class period would be spent on students working independently on some type of worksheet or bookwork. The bell rang, that group left, a new group of students came in, and the process would start again. This seemed familiar.

Honestly, I didn't think this was very engaging or innovative education. However, the students were extremely well-behaved and seemed to appreciate the structure of the class. They always knew what to expect and I remember thinking that it really seemed to work. I took lots of notes as I observed him teach, both on what he was doing and what I would do differently.

Of course, because I was student teaching, I had a chance to prepare and teach a few lessons of my own. Because of the very specific structure of the class, I was told that I would need to adhere to his patterned teaching. I developed a series of lessons on topics that were based on the text and I carried out the agreed upon formula: assessment, lecture, worksheet, goodbye, and repeat. I was fairly pleased with my ability to implement this structure and received some positive feedback.

It was during the lecture portion of the lessons where I shined. I would lecture by trying to tell good stories and use humor to engage the students. I also tried my best to solicit student feedback and responses during the lecture. I would ask students questions as I navigated the content, in an attempt to keep them engaged and integrate their perspectives into the stories. This is fairly easy to do in social studies because all the content is already a story, so it allows for ample opportunities to ask questions like, "What do you think happened," "What would you have done," or "How would this work today?"

My most vivid memory from this student teaching placement was when I was required to video record one of my lessons. I checked out a camera (back in 2003 video cameras were not on phones yet) and a tripod from the media center at Maryville College. I put the tape into the camera (yes, tape), set it up in the back left of the room and filmed one of my 45-minute lessons. I was then required to bring that tape back to the college and watch it with my advisor to reflect and self-evaluate. The point was to discover how I was actually doing, not just how I thought I was doing. That's an important distinction.

The process was absolutely awful. We sat down in front of a big TV, plugged in the camera and pressed play. I was so uncomfortable watching myself teach. My immediate thought was that I looked terrible on video. My clothes and hair looked bad. Beyond that, I was rambling quite a bit, gesturing wildly while talking way too fast and using "uh" and "all right" as fillers between every sentence. I would describe being forced to watch myself teach as torture. It caused so much cognitive dissonance[3] (what I was seeing on screen was different than what I believed about myself) that I basically tuned it out. I "watched" most of the video staring past the TV, fixating on a poster on the wall that had a picture of an apple. Under the apple, it read, "Teachers Shape Lives."

Recently, and I think due to the rise of Marvel and DC comic book movies, there is a statement that has become popular with teachers. I have seen "Teaching is my Superpower" on mugs, t-shirts, and posters in classrooms and workrooms all over the country. This type of statement is nothing new. I have seen oodles of t-shirts, mugs and posters over the past 15 years that have similar sentiments like, "Teachers shape lives" and "Teachers are miracle workers." Society desires that teachers step into classrooms and perform incredible feats with whatever salary, resources, and conditions they are given. How was I going to be a superhero, shape lives or work miracles if I was unable to even look at myself?

I had to look away because when I watched the video it made me feel like a failure. Watching myself teach was unequivocally convincing me that I was a terrible teacher. After the video was over, my advisor gave me some positive and critical feedback. Honestly, I was so traumatized that I was not even really listening. I simply agreed with everything he said and vowed to work on the things that he outlined. I got out of that room as fast as I could, thinking that I never ever wanted to watch myself teach again,

---

3 Merriam-Webster: Psychological conflict resulting from incongruous beliefs and attitudes held simultaneously.

convinced that the camera somehow didn't project my superhero powers. I got back to the shed and my hands were shaking from the trauma.

The three weeks at Maryville Middle School seemed to go by quickly and before I knew it, it was time to transition to Maryville High School, which was right across the street. The first few days were spent observing Mr. Norris' class. He was the only economics teacher at the school and this is what I saw. He would start the class period with an assessment (some type of quiz), and then he would lecture for 50 minutes. Finally, he would assign bookwork or a worksheet for students to complete for the rest of the class period. This was the pattern each day. Does this seem familiar? At least things were consistent.

Economics was my main area of interest and what I wanted to (and would eventually) teach. Therefore, I was absolutely interested in spending my entire student teaching experience in this economics classroom. Mr. Norris told me that I was welcome to do so, taking over all of his economics classes. He also said that he would be totally supportive of me trying new teaching techniques with the students. This is exactly what I wanted. I was very excited about the opportunity.

TURMOIL

The head of the social studies department at Maryville High School, Mrs. Yates, was a "liaison" for Maryville College. That meant she was in control of directing and placement of college students (like me) working with social studies teachers at the high school. I had decided that I was going to spend my student teaching placement with Mr. Norris. Unbeknownst to me, before I met with her, Mrs. Yates had decided that I was going to spend half of my placement in Mr. Norris' economics classroom and the other half in Mr. Wilder's American History classroom. These two unilateral decisions were expressed in a heated meeting one morning during second period in Mrs. Yates' room.

I was under the impression that this meeting was to let her know about my plans to carry out my entire placement with Mr. Norris. I told her that I preferred spending as much time as possible in that placement because it would give me more time to try different teaching techniques. She disagreed, stating that having a more diverse student teaching experience would make it easier for me to find a job. If I remember correctly, I said something like, "I don't care about finding a job, I care about having the best opportunity to improve my skill as a teacher." That didn't go over well, at all.

We got into a full-blown argument right there in her classroom, during her planning period. I was 25 years old and she was treating me like a high schooler. At this point in my life, I had a hard time finding humor in these types of situations (nowadays, I would find it hysterical). I said a few additional choice statements that made it clear that I did not respect her authority. And she said a few statements in retort. The argument ended with me cutting her off mid-sentence, thanking her (sarcastically) for her time and saying that I would simply go back to the college and they would handle it for me. She was visibly angry. I was angry. I left the room.

I did exactly what I said I was going to do. I got into my car, drove two miles to the college, went into the education office and waited (sitting in an uncomfortable wooden, creaky chair) to chat with the department head, who happened to be my advisor. When entering the room, I could tell he had already received a call about this issue.

Still, I opened the conversation saying something about paying lots of money to take these classes, and that I should have the opportunity to walk the path I want to walk. His response seemed condescending. He said that I needed to do what people told me to do because they know what is best for me. I didn't react well to that and slipped into my second argument of the day. Again, at that time, in my youth, I lacked the ability to find humor in these types of emotionally charged situations. I got quite upset. So did my advisor.

The next day I went back to the high school to begin my 10 weeks of student teaching. Half of the time was to be spent in Mr. Norris' economics class and the other half in Mr. Wilder's American History class. I completely lost that battle and only accomplished ticking off two people who had a hand in whether I would complete this licensure program. We will get back to that fallout in a minute.

The first few times I observed Mr. Wilder's history class, I saw that he would give the students an assessment to kick off the period. Then, he would lecture for 30 to 45 minutes. Finally, he would give a worksheet or bookwork for the students to complete for the rest of the class period. Ah, the pattern.

Now, to be perfectly clear, I was not judging the pattern. Actually, it was what I was used to seeing most of my life. And let's remember that for me the solution to educational issues, at the time, was wrapped up in the personality of the teacher, not so much in the pedagogy. This makes sense because I had never experienced a different approach to teaching and learning. Therefore, when I chose to adopt this pattern of instruction, it was justifiable.

I was convinced that I was doing a better job than other teachers simply because I was bringing my stellar personality into the room. Who I was as a person, how much I cared, and my ability to "connect" with students allowed me to provide a high-quality education.

I enjoyed my student teaching experience at Maryville High School. Mr. Norris and Mr. Wilder were great and allowed me to try new teaching strategies. However, you will not be surprised that most of my instruction consisted of assessment, lecture, and bookwork.

Toward the end of my time teaching the economics class, I wanted to try something new. I had been a musician most of my life and was also a song-writer. I had my Nashville mobile recording studio in the shed (yup, I am still living there through all these shenanigans), so I decided that I was going to write a song about one of the topics we were studying in class. Thus, I wrote and recorded a song about diminishing marginal utility, the rule that as you consume more of a good, the utility or pleasure diminishes on the margin. For example, if you have eight slices of pizza and are extremely hungry, the first slice is going to provide a lot of utility/pleasure. The fourth slice will have less utility than the first and the eighth slice might have very little utility.

My lesson plan for this song was simple. I played the track for the students. We read and discussed the meaning of the lyrics. Then I rolled in my recording studio to document the students singing the song along with the track. After we sang and recorded it, I remixed the song with all the voices and played it again for the students. The project took about a period and a half and the students seemed to really enjoy the process. A few of them who had been disengaged during my other lessons (lectures) were out of their seats, dancing around and singing along.

I remember thinking that this was a great lesson, but that it had two serious flaws. First, it took too long. Second, it was a review of previously covered content. It gave the students a unique learning experience, but took up too much class time for just reinforcing one concept. It was a neat and engaging lesson, but it was not a scalable teaching technique. There was no way I could repeat it for all the concepts I was required to teach.

ALTERNATIVES

While I was student teaching, I was also taking my master's classes at the University of Tennessee (UT) in downtown Knoxville, about a 20-minute drive from Maryville. Not surprisingly, most of the classes consisted of listening to lectures punctuated by some discussion. Some of the courses were interesting and I did enjoy reading education research and thinking deeply about teaching and learning theories. It gave me a chance to discover concepts that aligned with and strengthened my ideas.[4] Now that I had a handful of days of classroom experience, my self-righteousness continued to rule my thoughts about teaching and learning.

Similar to my undergrad licensure program at Maryville, my classes at UT gave me an opportunity not only to think about classroom strategies, but also allowed me to write about them. I found that I enjoyed writing (which is probably not surprising given that you are reading this). I would write passionately about a range of topics – from vouchers to standardized testing – and then contribute in an outspoken manner if those topics were brought up during class time.

I was especially fascinated with thinking about and discussing alternative assessment strategies. I wrote multiple papers arguing for the adoption of more holistic assessments (ways of determining whether students learned the content) like portfolios or projects. I did not believe that the typical testing strategies that were used in most schools measured the most important parts of learning. They didn't measure whether the students were developing a love of learning or if they appreciated learning because of the efforts of the teacher. I think it was the latter that bothered me the most. I had a hard time thinking that my value as a teacher would be assessed by student scores on multiple choice tests, especially when we could assess students in different ways that required them to be engaged in creating something valuable.

Student teaching allowed me to develop and experiment with a few alternative assessment techniques. My favorite strategy was extremely simple. Instead of a test at the end of the chapter on inflation and recession, I had the students prepare a two-minute speech that they would be able to communicate if this topic came up in conversation. Their speech had to concisely cover the most important information found in the chapter.

---

4 That's called confirmation bias.

I had 25 students in my econ class, so one-by-one each stepped out in the hallway, where I was sitting, and delivered their speech. I graded them on their understanding of the content as well as their communication skills. This was challenging for all the students, and it was a great way for me to know if they really understood the basics before we moved on to the next chapter. With the few minutes left at the end of the period, I invited the two students who I thought gave the best speeches to deliver them again in front of the class. This was a much better assessment of student understanding than a multiple-choice test.

During my student teaching placement at Maryville High School, the students frequently told me that they thought I was crazy because I did things differently. In all fairness, I was doing things differently to *stop* from going crazy from the monotonous process of the education that I had received my whole life. I was trying to be like Mr. Mott and Mrs. Thornhill by creating an exciting learning environment, showing students my unique personality, that I cared, and offering them different ways to get involved in the content.

Of course, I also met all the technical requirements for student teaching. All the students in the licensure program were required to create a binder of lesson plans that would be graded at the end of the semester. In addition, I had to be observed multiple times by a college representative. These observations were "graded" using a rubric. All my observations received excellent marks.

I received an A on my binder because everything was in order and completed. I followed all the rules. However, I received a B in student teaching, which did not make any sense. The only objective evidence of my student teaching performance were my observations. All my observations were completed, and each received top scores. In fact, to my knowledge, everyone who received an A on the binder also received an A in student teaching except for me. So, what happened? Oh, you can probably guess.

I got super angry and wanted to find out the reason for this outrageous occurrence. Once again, I stormed into the education office at the college and waited to meet with my advisor in that uncomfortable chair. When called, I shuffled into his office with my binder and said, "How is it possible to get an A on all the requirements of students teaching, but to get a B in student teaching?" His response enraged me. He simply said, "Sometimes you just have to accept things that happen."

Surely this was fallout from my earlier dust up with Mrs. Yates. Well, I thought, that certainly won't stand. I sarcastically thanked him for his time and hard work and dramatically exited the office. I immediately walked over to the office of the dean of students and waited in a fancy oversized chair for a chance to talk to her. I pleaded my case, explaining all the pertinent details, and she said, "You can make a formal complaint, or you can just ignore it and move on. Getting a B in student teaching will have no impact on your career as a teacher."

The formal complaint process was just a bunch of paperwork that I would need to fill out and I was told that it was basically like adding a suggestion to the suggestion box at the DMV. Sure, they read those suggestions, but is anyone going to do anything about it? Probably not. Pragmatically, I chose to let it go and move on, but have and probably always will carry a significant amount of bitterness about this issue. I felt like this education program was lucky to have a passionate teacher like me, and I didn't understand why I would be treated this way. Poor me.

Incidentally, a decade later I won Maryville College's Kin Takashi Award for Young Alumni for my contributions and work in education. It took everything in me to not add the statement "not bad for someone who got a B in student teaching" in my acceptance speech.[5] Instead, I talked about how much I appreciated everything college had done for me, which was absolutely true.

---

5 Kin Takahashi Award. Retrieved from http://schooled.lodgemccammon.com

CHAPTER 5

My First Teaching Job

• • •

I FINISHED THE TEACHING PROGRAM at Maryville College in May 2003 with straight A's (except for my B in student teaching). In June, I took and passed the Praxis exam to receive my teaching license for 7-12 social studies. In early July, I completed the requirements for my master's degree in education with a focus in instructional technology from the University of Tennessee. I had finished all of this in 14 months, and it felt good to be successful and have a purpose.

My parents were in town for the 4th of July holiday and I remember being in the kitchen at my sister's house with my mom, bragging that I had finished all the requirements for my licensure and master's, and probably also lamenting the B in student teaching. She replied, "Well, I suppose you should look for a job."

Before that moment, it never even occurred to me that I would need to look for a job. In fact, I remember clearly telling Mrs. Yates that I didn't care about getting a job, only about getting better at teaching.

Spending three and a half years in a shed didn't exactly prepare me for the job hunt. Honestly, I thought my mom was being a little insensitive. I mean, the fact that I had completed anything at all (beyond playing tennis and eating soup) was amazing, and all she could think about was me finding a job. But I guess she was right.

Having absolutely no idea how to look for a teaching job (or any type of job for that matter), I walked into the office of my sister's house and got on her computer. I opened Internet Explorer and went to Google. I paused there, thinking about where I might like to work. I recalled a conversation that I had a few years before with my good friend Todd, when he said that he really liked North Carolina. I'm not sure why that detail jumped out at me in that moment, but it did. I Googled, "Capital of North Carolina." The result, of course, was Raleigh. Then, I Googled, "School district Raleigh NC." The result was Wake County. I then Googled, "High school teaching jobs Wake Country." Google corrected my misspelling and asked me if I meant Wake County? Oh, yes, I did mean that. It was embarrassing to misspell a Google search when looking for a teaching job. Luckily, no one else was around.

The first link that Google suggested was a page on the North Carolina Department of Public Instruction's website for current high school teacher openings in Wake County. That seemed to be a good place to start. It was a long list of jobs on a single page. The third position posted on the list was for an AP Economics teacher at Wakefield High School, and next to the position title it directed me to send a resume to the principal, Mr. Smith.

One of my licensure classes had required me to create a resume. At the time, I had found that to be a hassle; however, in this moment, I realized that it was a very practical assignment. I attached my resume to an email and sent it along to Mr. Smith. In the second that it took for the email to disappear after hitting send, I wondered how I might explain a four-year gap in my school or work history. I had not participated in anything structured since the summer of 1999 when I was in recording classes in Hollywood for two weeks. I figured that truth was more entertaining than any fiction I could manufacture. I would tell whoever asked, that I lived in a shed to find myself and to avoid law school.

Meanwhile, back in reality, it had been less than 10 minutes since my mom had asked me about finding a job. I walked back into the kitchen, sat down, and said, "I applied for a job."

Exactly 53 minutes after I sent that email to Mr. Smith, he sent a short reply asking if I could call him, so we could talk further about the position. He included his phone number, so I called right away. I had already figured out what to say about the shed, so I was totally prepared for anything.

We chatted on the phone like we were old buddies for about 15 minutes. He didn't ask about the four-year gap or the shed. At the end of the conversation, he asked if I could come visit the school the following day for a more formal interview. I said that would not be a problem.

I walked back into the kitchen and told my mom, "I have an interview tomorrow in North Carolina." That all happened over the course of about an hour. I didn't realize at the time that this was unusual. I thought finding a teaching job was super-duper simple.

That night I drove east out of the foothills of the Smoky Mountains, across the Appalachian range and into the piedmont region, arriving in Raleigh shortly after one in the morning. I had never been there before, and I didn't know where to stay. In 2003, I didn't have internet on my Nokia 3560, so I followed my printed MapQuest directions to the school. Once I arrived, I drove around until I found a hotel. The first one I found was the Super 8 on Capital Boulevard, approximately 10 miles away. It was not luxurious, but decidedly nicer than the shed.

The next morning (really, later that morning) I showed up at the school for my interview. It was extremely hot and humid, which is typical for July in North Carolina. I was wearing a button-down short-sleeve shirt tucked into khakis with a brown leather belt and leather shoes. My entire outfit was brand new since I didn't really have any respectable clothes. During college I was not known for my fashion sense and life in the shed did not have a dress code. Luckily, before I left, my mom took me to the mall and set me up. Best. Parents. Ever.

I chatted with Mr. Smith for 30 minutes about music, traveling in Russia (I played in my mother's Suzuki music group and we toured Russia in 1991) and the weather. It was a very relaxed conversation. Then, we took a walk around the school and chatted a bit about the student and teacher population. As he was talking, I was in some sort of daze. I was reeling at the thought that 14 months before I had no clue what I wanted to do with my life. Now, I had done all this education stuff and was walking through high school hallways on a job interview to be a teacher. I mean, who in the world would hire me as a teacher and give me a classroom? I had decided to teach out of nowhere, largely because I needed something to do and could not think of anything else. Surely, he would see right through me and know that I was not remotely qualified to teach at this school.

I had been there about an hour when we found ourselves back in his office. He said, "How would you like to come work here?" I said, "I would like that." That was that. I just got my first teaching job.

I drove back to Maryville, packed up the shed, rented an apartment in Raleigh, and two weeks later my first group of students walked into my classroom. I was convinced that I would be wildly successful because the students were going to connect with my personality. They were all going to say, "Mr. McCammon is great. He inspires me to want to learn."

CHAPTER 6
Mr. McCammon

• • •

I AM MR. MCCAMMON. WELCOME to my life. This will be way different than living in the shed. Here is my classroom. Here are my textbooks. Here is my pacing guide. You may be wondering, "What is a pacing guide?" It's a document created by the school district to ensure that all teachers and students are covering the same topic on the same day across different classrooms and schools. It's very specific how many days you have to cover specific topics. It does not matter if you think certain topics are more important or interesting than others. Just follow the pacing guide and you'll be fine.

For a new teacher, a pacing guide is a valuable resource. Having a built-in, clear structure and series of expectations means that being a "good" teacher is also clear and achievable. To be a successful social studies teacher at Wakefield High School, all I needed to do was follow the rules. I thought back to the interview with my professors at Maryville College where they told me that I would struggle because it seemed like I didn't want to follow the rules. Well, those were the same folks who gave me, the one with superhero teaching powers, a B in student teaching. What do they know? Surely, I could follow these new guidelines.

So, off we go. Wakefield High School ran on block scheduling just like Maryville High School, meaning that I taught three 90-minute classes/blocks each day. I taught two blocks of Civics and Economics (C&E) and one block of AP Economics (APECON). C&E was a required course for sophomores and APECON was an elective, mainly filled with seniors and a few juniors.

The exhaustion of having my own classes all day every day hit me like a ton of bricks. Teaching for 270 minutes each day while managing 30 teenagers is physically and mentally demanding. Since my whole "I know better than anyone else what will solve the problems of education" theory depended largely upon my personality being the cornerstone of my teaching, I quickly became aware of the fact that my personality (enthusiasm, humor, patience, etc.) was the first thing that suffered when I was overly tired. That was a serious problem because I didn't have many pedagogical strategies to fall back on.

My training programs did not provide me with many practical strategies that allowed me to succeed in offering a great education for all my students. Most of the strategies I learned were things that might work in classrooms where teachers are not exhausted and have ample time to experiment. During student teaching at Maryville High School, I was not exhausted and had time to experiment because I split the instruction load with my cooperating teachers. They allowed me to move at whatever pace I wanted, and they gave me lots of freedom to experiment with their classes. My actual teaching job at Wakefield was totally different. I had this pacing guide and was responsible for every instructional minute of every day, in addition to an avalanche of additional administrative responsibilities like grading and meetings.

When I did try my various alternative teaching strategies, I found I would fall behind the pacing guide. Now that I was in my own classroom, it seemed that I didn't have time to deviate from the traditional heavy lecture method because anything else took too long to implement. I was even told a few times by mentor teachers that I needed to "stick to covering the content." I was now starting to understand why I had spent my entire school life listening to lectures. It seemed that other strategies don't quite fit into the public school mold.

After about a month, I settled into my teaching rhythm. The students would come in. I would give an assessment. Then, I would lecture for 45 to 60 minutes. With the remaining class time, I would assign a worksheet or have them do problems out of the book that reinforced the content from the lecture. Sometimes I allowed them to work together on these assignments. Again, this is what I had seen my entire school career and I really started to learn more about the merits of this traditional teaching method. It's the best way to control a group of students. It's the best way to stay with the pacing guide. It's the best way to stay sane during such an exhausting day-to-day pace. Teaching like this allows you to just switch on the autopilot and coast.

Just like during student teaching, this strategy worked pretty well for me. It allowed me to automate the pedagogy of teaching, while I intermittently took advantage of my personality. I was well liked. My students thought I was smart, caring, interesting, nice and funny. I considered myself to be a successful teacher. I was showing up and following the rules.

While this class structure allowed me to coast a bit, I did have an issue. I really disliked repeating myself. I would give my 50-minute lecture in block one and then repeat the same thing for block two and then again in block four. All three lectures were quite inconsistent. The lecture during block one was rough because it was first thing in the morning and I was tired. The lecture in block two was much better because I had already been through it. The lecture in block four was brutal because I was tired of talking, so I would skip parts.

After I gave an assessment to find out what the students remembered from my previous lecture, I would usually have to give a shortened version of the same lecture to patch up the gaps resulting from my inconsistency. This mind-numbing repetition exhausted me. At the end of the day, I would collapse into my chair, frustrated by the thought that I was spending so much time telling students stuff that many won't remember tomorrow.

After a few months, I had to change it up. I was starting to get bored with my lesson structure and I assumed that the students were feeling the same way. I really wanted to be innovative and try some new things. I decided to attempt a strategy that I had developed during student teaching, but that was not on the pacing guide. I wrote and recorded a song called "The Party Party" about the political party system that I could use to reinforce the content in my C&E classes.

After my lecture about political parties, I played "The Party Party" for my students, and then we talked about the lyrics and their meaning. The lyrics contained some vocabulary, but also required explication to get at some of the deeper meaning in the content. This ensured that the lyrics would be more than a mnemonic device. I wanted the lyrics to spark discussion. So, we discussed the lyrics as a class and it worked pretty well. We listened to the song a few times and I eventually got the students singing along.

Once the classes knew the song well enough, I took them down to the media center and had each student get on a computer to research and write a report about a third party. Meanwhile, I pulled small groups of students into a classroom attached to the media center. In that classroom, I set up the mobile recording studio with six sets of headphones. Each student put on a set of headphones and sang along with the song while I recorded their voices. This was basically the same process that I had used at Maryville High School to have the students sing the song about diminishing marginal utility. However, I also video recorded each group's performance. After doing this with all my classes (in addition to some students from other classes who heard about the project and wanted to participate), we had a song with over 100 voices singing about political parties.

I went home and cut together an "in the studio" style music video of their performance. It was not fancy, but I made sure that every student was featured. Think of a "We are the World" type video, but with students singing in unison about political parties.

The final product was pretty incredible. It was an artifact of both learning and an engaging activity. The video showed complete student engagement, but instead of unveiling the video to my classes the next day, I gave the finished version to the Wakefield morning news and had them broadcast it into every classroom during the announcements at the beginning of second period. This music video received a good amount of positive feedback from students, teachers and the administration. It was a lot of fun and a valuable experience. But then came the sobering reality.

We spent about a day too long, per the pacing guide, on political parties. Engaging students with this alternative teaching strategy had a very real and immediate consequence. It meant that the following day, I said to my classes, "OK, buckle up. Because we spent too much time on political parties and recording our video, we need to get through a ton of information today. I am going to lecture for 75 minutes so we can catch back up."

That day was the worst. I talked the students and myself into a trance, repeating that same 75-minute lecture multiple times. But we had to catch up somehow.

Side note: I would like to share the diminishing marginal utility song and The Party Party music video, but they have been lost in the shuffle of moving files across computers and hard drives over the years. Back in 2003, we did not have the cloud for storing digital content nor did we have anything like YouTube.

From time to time, my classes could be seen making music videos, working on projects in the computer lab or playing monopoly with alternative rules to demonstrate topics like monetary or fiscal policy. Those were the fun days. However, every day that followed was brutal because we had to pay for the fun with a lengthy catch-up lecture to cover the content. I wanted to have more days that were focused on student engagement, but I was not able to figure out how. The pacing guide was always telling me to hurry up, and it was constantly reminding me that I was not following the rules.

The exhausting pace of the classroom, in addition to being bummed that I was not able to figure out how to engage my students every day started to grind me down. It wore me out, and as I became worn, my personality (the perceived core element of my value as a teacher) started to diminish. Over time I became less patient, funny and energetic. Mrs. Thornhill and Mr. Mott would have been so disappointed. I was failing them, and I was failing myself.

The Sunshine Committee

It didn't make me feel better, but this same stress and exhaustion was happening all throughout the school. Most teachers seemed to be suffering in similar ways. I knew this because at the beginning of my second year I was asked to be the head of the Sunshine Committee at Wakefield High School. The committee had three responsibilities. First, make sure sympathy cards were delivered when faculty or staff had a loss in the family. Second, plan the holiday parties. Last, and most important, spread sunshining happiness throughout the building every day.

Spreading happiness was essential because everyone was stressed, and I totally got it. I frequently described teaching as having 500 things to do at any given moment, but only having the time to do five of them. As a result, I noticed a trend that overall job satisfaction among the faculty and staff seemed to decrease every day. By the end of the year, pretty much everyone was out of his or her minds and needed a summer break to stay sane.

It made sense why this was happening. Everyone was trying to get through the content, repeating him or herself into oblivion. Even though it was only my second year teaching and I was drowning probably more than most, I considered it my mission to try to improve each day for my colleagues by spreading some "sunshine." It was a difficult task, and I am not sure if I was successful beyond generating some laughs and happiness.

The committee, made up mostly of my teacher friends, immediately implemented two tactics in the attempt to improve job satisfaction. We were supposed to collect donations to pay for all the Sunshine Committee activities (parties, gifts). In the past, members just went door to door asking teachers to pay $10. I tried a new tactic. I wanted to get people to come to us with their donation and spread a little sunshine at the same time.

We did this by putting signs in the faculty bathrooms, reminding people to pay their sunshine dues. These were not just regular signs. I did a Google image search for "Ray" (like ray of sunshine) and grabbed the first picture that I found. That picture was on every Sunshine Committee notice that we posted around the school. Funny thing was that the first picture on Google was of an elderly man wearing a white sleeveless t-shirt. I assumed his name was Ray, which is why it came up in the search. Regardless, that was our mascot. An elderly man named Ray was put on all the posters, which read, "Ray says, don't forget to pay your Sunshine Committee dues."

Side note: I would post a picture of Ray, but I don't actually have one, nor do I know who he was. I would hate to put a random person's picture in my book and them find out.

Within a day, everyone in the school was talking about Ray. Within three days, almost everyone in the school had paid. They came to us to give their $10, but also to find out more about Ray. We made up lots of stories about who he was to keep people guessing. The bathroom "Ray says" campaign worked so well for fundraising and spreading happiness that we kept it going.

Over the next few months, we kept posting signs in the bathrooms that said things like, "Ray says, vitamin D is the bestest" and "Ray says, the government can make video cameras the size of a pin." We might have gone a little too far, but generally people found it all quite funny. Some, not so much. But you can't please everyone, especially math teachers (it was mostly the math teachers who would tear down the posters in the bathrooms and complain about their existence).

I felt like we were increasing job satisfaction a little, but I wanted to do more. The second strategy that some members of the committee (mostly me and my good friend John who was a chemistry teacher) initiated involved going around the school during our planning periods and offering our fellow teachers hugs. Of course, we did not force hugs on anyone, but we popped into every classroom and would offer. The best hugs were when a teacher was mid-lecture with a room full of students. Many hug recipients would say something like, "You made my day." That was the goal.

LEAVING

I was certainly not shielded from the stresses of teaching, and I could have used more sunshine (laughing and hugs) myself. Toward the end of the fall semester of 2004, during my second year, the grind of teaching broke down my health. I got bronchitis and I could not shake it. I slowly got worse over the course of a month until one night I woke up and was having trouble breathing. A friend drove me to the emergency room.

I was out of school for three weeks as I healed from a series of medical issues brought on by sickness, stress and exhaustion. Over those three weeks, I decided that I was not strong enough to teach. Maybe it was too much going from the shed to such a structured environment. Maybe I expected too much of myself. Maybe I am weak. Maybe all of those things. Regardless, I was going to finish out the year and then transition to something else. I called my dad and asked him what I should do, and he said, "If you don't know what to do, go to law school." Just kidding. That didn't happen again.

What did happen is that I finished the school year. It was still quite stressful, but I dialed the intensity back a bit. It was more important not to end up in the hospital than it was to not be constantly disappointed in myself for doing a poor job at engaging my students every single day. I went into survival mode. I did fewer projects, more lecturing and more worksheets. Teaching had broken me, or so I thought.

One spring afternoon, during my last semester in 2005, we had a social studies department meeting. On this particular day, Mr. Smith was going around to all the department meetings in order to discuss some "critical information." The No Child Left Behind law had been put into place in 2001 and I had heard it mentioned many times in faculty and district meetings. Each time someone brought it up, it was followed by platitudes like, "We really need to work toward pulling up scores" or "We need to do a better job at preparing students for these new tests." Those are platitudes because I had heard them so many times that they lost their meaning, and because nobody offered any guidance for *how* to solve the problem of low test scores. Essentially, those platitudes suggested that teachers needed to do a "better" job. At the time, it seemed like the school leaders were saying, "Hey, we know you are running as fast as you can, but we need you to run 10 percent faster."

In fact, this was why the principal was attending our department meeting, to tell us to run faster. He said two things that completely broke my spirit and allowed me to justify leaving Wakefield at the end of the 2005 school year.

First, he said, "If it's not your first priority to increase student test scores, you don't belong here." He went on to describe the type of teaching that increases student test scores. You guessed it. We were reminded to relentlessly stick to the pacing guide and county materials. I fundamentally disagreed with this sentiment. I saw my role as doing my best to inspire students to love learning, even though I had not figured out how to do it without ending up in the hospital. Regardless, that was my priority. In fact, I felt like student test scores increased when I deviated from that pacing guide. The second thing he said was, "It's not like 20 years ago, when we could waste time in school singing songs." Ouch. Was that intentionally directed at me?

Mr. Smith's pep talk convinced me to go back to school. While my motivation to pursue more schooling was based on a number of reasons, ultimately, it was because I was wrong about my solution to the problems of education. Having a great personality is not the solution. It's really nice to have a winning personality, but if you only have that and no real pedagogical skills to offer, teacher impact will be limited.

Also, personality is not scalable. It's difficult to teach someone to have the "right" personality for a job. Therefore, even if we all agreed that was the answer, we would not be able to easily spread it to other teachers. In fact, it was extremely egotistical to think that my personality was the solution. I was young and overly enthusiastic about being out of the shed. I didn't know any better.

However, it makes perfect sense that I felt that way. For some reason, I had to think that I was the answer. I believe many teachers feel this way to a certain extent. We need to feel like we are the model that should be replicated. We think that our love, caring and compassion will change the world. Heck, we've seen it printed on t-shirts and coffee mugs! And we have to think that, otherwise why would we do this crazy job? However, I wanted to move past believing that just caring a lot was enough, so I was ready to apply for a Ph.D. program.

BACK TO SCHOOL

In the spring semester of 2005, while wrapping up my time at Wakefield, I applied for acceptance into the College of Education's Ph.D. program at North Carolina State University (NCSU) with a focus in instructional technology. A week after I applied, I was contacted by the News and Observer, the biggest local newspaper in Raleigh. They wanted to write a story on the music-based pedagogy that I was intermittently using in my classroom to engage students. A reporter and photographer came to my house, where I had a small recording studio, and talked to me about the process of educational songwriting and the merits of using music in the classroom. A few days later the article came out, and I dropped by a gas station on my way to school and grabbed a copy (OK, I grabbed a few). Throughout the day, a number of my students walked in the room and said that they had seen the article and picture in the paper that morning. A bunch of parents emailed and said they saw it, and told me that they were happy that their child was in my class. Nice.

The most interesting and significant impact of that article was that I received an email from Dr. Carol, education professor at NCSU. She had read the article and wanted to talk with me. I met her and Dr. Candy at

Candy's house a few days later. While there, surrounded by what seemed like hundreds of Russian nesting dolls (she traveled to and from Russia studying their schools), we chatted about education, research and my professional goals.

Now that I think of it, the first 30 minutes of conversation when I interviewed with Mr. Smith for my teaching position almost two years earlier was largely about Russia. Once again, I was regaling potential employers with stories of when I traveled to Russia with the chamber orchestra. I even wowed them with a few Russian words that I remembered from studying it for three years in high school.

That detail seemed significant because, unbeknownst to me, I was in another interview surrounded by all these dolls. Dr. Carol and Dr. Candy were interviewing me to determine if they wanted to be my advisors for a Ph.D. program at NCSU. After a short conversation, they asked if I would like to work with them on my degree with a focus in curriculum development.

They told me that they had seen my application and noticed that I asked to be admitted into the instructional technology program, but that the college was currently searching for professors to fill vacancies in that department. Thus, my application had been literally placed on the rejection pile. However, Dr. Carol and Dr. Candy (in the department of curriculum development) told me that they happened to see my article in the News and Observer, recognized my name from the application and wanted to work with me. They also offered me an assistantship. Beyond paying for my school, this assistantship would allow me to work with them for 20 hours each week on their grant-funded research projects. I said, "yes."

I finished up my semester at Wakefield knowing what was next, and knowing that I would have a new venue that would support my interest in finding a different solution to the problems of education.

CHAPTER 7

Becoming Dr. Lodge

• • •

For all intents and purposes, it could be argued that teaching had been my second major failure, after the whole LSAT debacle. I had approached the profession with over-the-top arrogance and convinced myself that my unique and beautiful personality was going to be the solution to the problems in education, which honestly does not make a lot of sense. I figured that Mrs. Thornhill and Mr. Mott made my education experience exceptional, so we simply needed more teachers like them. Thus, if I emulated them, I would be contributing to this solution. I know now that I was wrong, but was having a crisis of faith. Ray says, "What I believed so strongly had been dashed on the taupe walls of the high school hallways and bathrooms."

My failure as a teacher fueled an obsession in identifying the real solution to the problems in education. I needed to learn how to create a more engaging classroom experience for all students, every day. I had learned a little, but it was clear that I needed a more diverse range of information and experience, beyond just doing the same thing day-after-day in my high school classroom.

The university was a good place to continue my quest.

I Was Amazing, Believe Me

In the summer of 2005, immediately after I tendered my resignation from Wakefield High School, I began my courses in the Ph.D. program at NCSU. Boy oh boy was this a welcome change of pace! The relaxed, spaced out, slow-roasted, heady nature of the university was exactly what I needed. After two years of being on stage, charged with the responsibility of teaching 150 students and feeling like a failure because I could not figure out how to engage them, I was finally free.

It was also a very welcome change in environment because I was dead set on figuring out what went wrong with my teaching experience and developing a solution. I was on a mission. I wanted to use my economic reasoning skills to develop a simple model for how to knock this teaching thing out of the park.

My graduate classes thrust me back into the world of the theoretical. The information was delivered by professors who had either never been in a public school classroom or who had not been there in many years, even decades. The classes were taught in a similar way to most everything else I had experienced up to this point. I spent the majority of my time sitting and listening to lectures.

I didn't find this (in)activity overly distasteful or odd since I had perpetrated a very similar process in my recent high school classroom. However, I was a bit dismayed because I realized quickly that these professors were not going to be able to help me solve my problem. Simply put, if they knew how to engage students every day, they would be engaging us every day. Instead, they were lecturing every day.

Similar to all my past school experiences, the classes I liked the most were led by the professors I liked the most. The only discernable difference from class to class was the professor's personality. I found this frustrating because I had already discovered that personality was not the solution to educational problems. Sitting in chairs for hours listening to lectures was not going to help me achieve my mission. However, I did reconcile that attending these classes was better for my mental and physical health. Thus, I was still thrilled and energized to be there.

The next thing that happened, and it happened quickly, was that I became completely delusional about what kind of teacher I had been in the classroom and what impact I had on student learning. This was interesting because, just like when I was in my teacher training program three years before, I was now back to a similar mentality. I was re-convinced that my ideas were the gold standard and that teaching was my superhero power, now made worse by the fact that I had "teaching experience." My experience emboldened my self-righteousness.

In reality, I left the classroom a failure – unable to survive the rigors of the teaching profession nor able to figure out a formula for making my classroom highly successful and engaging. Despite that reality, as soon as I started this Ph.D. program, I wore my experience around my fragile ego like a medal. I immediately shifted my attitude from that of failure to that of arrogance and success. I couldn't help myself. I was extremely insecure about my shortcomings and could not face the truth at the time, and certainly didn't want anyone else to know that I was a failed teacher. Plus, there were not any videos online showing my teaching, so nobody (including myself) really knew what kind of teacher I had been.

The funny thing is that almost everyone around me did exactly the same thing. These classes were filled with unwavering, self-righteous former or current teachers desperately spewing their own personal agendas and qualifying those opinions by referring to the figurative medal hanging on their ego inscribed with "Teaching is my superpower."

Like many of my peers, I returned to school because I did not have the answers, but upon the onset of school, I immediately started arguing that I did have the answers. It was confusing, but it stems back to the same phenomenon that we previously explored. To admit out loud that I was a failure at teaching means that my own education failed, and that I am not as good as I think I am.

What made it even more bizarre was that we were all claiming that our gold standard teaching experience gave us credibility to claim that we had solutions; however, none of our solutions were remotely the same. Every one of us was constantly arguing a very specific and personal agenda, advocating that our approach to teaching was the answer to every question. What's the best way to reach students with special needs? The way I did it. What's the best way to deal with large class sizes? The way I did it. What's the best way to get students to be leaders? The way I did it. On and on.

When I was teaching high school, I followed the same pedagogical patterns that I saw my entire life with only a few exceptions. The main aspect of my teaching that made me different (other than my personality) was that I used music in different and unique ways. So, I championed the use of music in the classroom and built strategies around it to engage students. I was not able to use this strategy often because of the amount of time it took away from covering the content, but music-based teaching defined me. I convinced myself that I was a great teacher because I used this music-based teaching in the classroom. That became my agenda and main talking point.

Then, I started "manufacturing data" to prove that I was great and that my music-based teaching had an extremely positive impact on student learning and engagement. I convinced myself that "all my students were engaged by this" and that "test scores increased because of my efforts." I even told myself and others that using music in the classroom helped my students develop a love of learning. Then I would use that "manufactured data," mostly consisting of my memory and opinions, to push my agenda during discussions.

I would tell others that I knew how to engage students and would reference my music-based lessons as a gold standard example. I would even insinuate that if other teachers didn't consider using music-based strategies, then they were not teaching the right way. I suppose I needed to feel like I was good, even if I misled myself and others.

Many of my peers seemed to dive back into their own teaching experiences and pick something that they did well. They grabbed ahold of a strategy or aspect of their personality that made them unique. They manufactured their own data. They developed their own agenda and away they went, telling everyone, "If you are not doing what I did in the classroom, which made me great, you are doing it wrong." Imagine, if you will, a room full of those egos. It's a fascinating environment where a group of almost debilitatingly insecure people are arguing over their deluded personal agendas, each claiming superiority by citing their classroom experience as proof.

Insecure, ego-driven, deluded arrogance is both a great and a dangerous attitude to take into a Ph.D. program. It's great because it's very easy for your advisor to say to you, "OK. You seem to be convinced that the thing that made you great is a great thing to do. The next step is to develop a study to see if that is actually the case." In other words, now that you are in a Ph.D. program, you don't get to manufacture data anymore. Now, you have to provide an actual, justifiable, and quantifiable basis for your agenda. You can see how that's a good thing, right? Essentially, it's elevating the conversation. Instead of saying, "I was amazing, believe me," you learn to say, "Here is some actual research and data that shows the impact of what I do." Those are two very different statements. Please keep in mind that it's important to be able to say the first statement in order to focus enough to develop the second.

On the other hand, it is a dangerous attitude because there are a number of ways to manipulate educational research and data to get exactly the outcomes you desire - from having small sample sizes, to only selecting certain types of subjects, to knowingly (or unknowingly) selecting the data that supports your claims. It all happens and could be construed as a form of confirmation bias (a tendency to view evidence in a way that confirms one's existing beliefs or theories). It's not difficult to see why this happens. I was an insecure person who was desperate to prove that the things that I believed in, the things that made me a great educator, are actually great things. If given a chance, I would probably have favored only outcomes that aligned with my belief to ensure that I was proven right. Luckily, I didn't need to.

The reason I see this attitude as dangerous is because some of these passionate researchers will manipulate research and data to push their agendas in schools. They will use that information to try and force teachers to use certain strategies. When these teachers refuse to adhere to these changes, the passionate researchers feel justified in saying, "If you don't do what I say, you are both unintelligent and part of the problem." I have heard statements like these from my colleagues with doctorates. I am certainly not saying that all, or even the preponderance of educational research is like this, but I am saying that in my 15 years in the industry, I have seen it more than once.

Let's rewind for a moment back to Wakefield for an example. I recall attending a Wake County professional development workshop. During this workshop, a professor was hired to present on a collaborative strategy that she had developed as part of a grant. A few minutes into her presentation it became very clear that what she was sharing with us was not useful because the examples she was using to "sell" the idea demonstrated how it worked in classes of 10 or fewer students. She had collected data on how it worked in small classes. All of my classes (and everyone else's in the room) had more than 25 students. There is a monumental difference between having 10 students in a room versus 25.

I could tell that almost all the teachers stopped paying attention at this point. Many, like me, took out other work. She asked a few questions to the audience during her lecture and nobody offered a response, suggesting that nobody cared or was even paying attention. She seemed frustrated by this lack of interaction, so she said, "It is really important to build collaborative classroom experiences because students need these skills for the future." In response to this comment, a math teacher who was sitting next to me raised her hand and asked, "Could you explain how this would work in a math class with 30 students, because that is what I have." The professor seemed to be caught off-guard by this question and simply restated the findings of how it worked in their classes of 10 or fewer and then said, "It will work the same way if you take the time to try it." Yes. Time. But nobody has any.

Now fast forward back to the university. I distinctly remember a number of conversations with professors who did education research. Many of them had their own agendas and received grants to develop strategies and tools that promote certain teaching methods. Many of their grants required them to go into schools and do professional development for teachers, showing them how the tools and strategies worked. Many professors would facilitate these sessions, come back to the university and report that the teachers were not intelligent enough to understand their techniques, identifying that as the reason the methods were not implemented in the classroom. It's as if they were not able to look at themselves or their agendas critically. Instead, they blamed others for their ideas not being adopted.

We can start to see a disconnect between research and practice. This is nothing new, and it also happens in industries outside of education all the time. It is said that professors in general operate in the "Ivory Tower" and function in a world of intellectualism that many times is disconnected from the practical concerns and challenges of the real world. In the case of education, I understand firsthand how difficult it is to stay connected with "real" classrooms while at the university. Aside from simply not teaching anymore, there is also the problem of being swayed by hyperbolic thoughts of your own experience.

But let's turn our focus toward the positive because there were a lot of magically delicious things that happened in graduate school, which nudged me down the path to some incredible discoveries.

CHAPTER 8

Focus

• • •

NOT SURPRISINGLY, I DECIDED TO take my unique snowflake of a delusion (that I was, in fact, a good teacher) and study it. I witnessed the power of music in the classroom and believed that it was a key to engagement, motivation, and student success, but I didn't have any non-fiction research or data to back up my belief. Thus, it became my goal to obtain evidence that music was a powerful learning tool.

Not only did I decide to make music my research focus, I also got wrapped up in thinking that music, oh wonderful music, was the solution. You might be thinking, "Hey, you said you were delusional, convincing yourself that the thing you did that made you successful was manufactured." Yes, that is correct. But, I was still caught up in those thoughts back then. I had not realized that it came from a place of insecurity about my real abilities and failures or my ego-driven needs. All those realizations came much later. At that time, I set my sights on the fact that the problem with school was that there was not enough music in the classroom. After all, for years we had heard statements like, "Music is the universal language" while books like "The Mozart Effect" had hit the popular press, giving everyone the notion that music is a powerful force for good and learning. I believed those things and now I wanted more evidence to prove that I was right.

THE FRIDAY INSTITUTE

I was extremely fortunate to be given an assistantship, a 20-hour per week job doing a variety of tasks connected to a grant. In 2005, at the end of my first summer of graduate school, the grant team I was working with moved to a new building on Centennial Campus, a few miles away. I was super bummed to hear that we would all be required to leave our cramped little office in Poe Hall, where we were right across the street from a bunch of restaurants and bars. Plus, being on main campus meant that I could leave work, walk to my classes and walk back to work. I valued being centrally located.

Centennial Campus was the new, fancy, high-tech campus where the engineering buildings (NCSU is internationally known for having a great engineering program) could be found. Not only did the campus have academic buildings, but there were also high-tech companies that leased office space, combining a university learning environment with corporate work environments. For example, Red Hat, a technology company, had offices on Centennial Campus right across from the computer science academic buildings. It seemed like a very cool and innovative idea and the campus was set up in a similar way for education. Centennial Campus Middle (a Wake County Public School) and the building we were moving to were physically attached. The idea was that research and practice would be connected to try and avoid the ivory tower issues discussed earlier.

The Friday Institute for Educational Innovation (FI), named after former president of the North Carolina University System William Friday, was a new high-tech education think tank. A number of individuals, companies, and corporations had donated millions of dollars for the building to be erected and had stocked it with the newest technologies available in 2005. The state legislature also carved out a yearly operating budget of almost two million dollars to support the work of the institute. The goal of the FI was to develop and promote research-based and technology-enhanced strategies that improved teaching and learning throughout the state of North Carolina.

There was an official ribbon cutting ceremony in August 2005. This was the same day that we (myself and the other graduate students who worked on the grant) moved into our new office space at the FI. Again, most of us were not overly enthusiastic about being moved off main campus, so there was a general apathy for this change. Centennial Campus was the southernmost part of NCSU, nothing was walkable, and we had to drive five minutes to get to the closest place to eat, which was Subway. Eat fresh.

On this hot and humid North Carolina afternoon, I packed up all my gear, which fit nicely into one small cardboard box, and drove over to the FI, a 10-minute jaunt. The parking lot for the building was almost full, so I had to park a good distance away from the front door. I grabbed my cardboard box and started walking. As I shuffled across that radiating asphalt, I thought of two years before when I was walking across a similar parking lot toward Wakefield High School for the first time. Now, I was walking toward a new building that would hold a series of new challenges and opportunities.

I quickly snapped back to reality. After about 30 yards, I noticed a large number of people collected in front of the entrance for the ribbon-cutting event. There were roughly 200 people wearing blue and black suits celebrating the coronation of this building. I was wearing shorts that were perhaps a little too tight and a t-shirt that was a little too baggy. As I approached this crowd of seemingly important (and certainly over-dressed) people, I realized quickly that I did not have the proper attire to blend in. Thus, I retraced my steps back to my car before being seen by too many attendees, and scurried around to the side entrance, with my cardboard box packed with marshmallow guns and picture frames. I had almost ruined the ribbon-cutting ceremony and concurrent speeches about how this building was, in fact, a solution to the problems of education in North Carolina. At that moment, I felt like I might be in the right place. All I needed was a blue (or black) suit.

SKEPTICAL

I had a number of opportunities to use music in the classroom while working at the FI, largely because it helped with my research. I would frequently work with teachers and students from the middle school next door, developing a variety of strategies that would eventually be used together in the design of music-based lessons. I also had the opportunity to use advanced technology resources to explore other ways of engaging students.

Being connected to a middle school was the best design ever for an education think tank. If I had an idea, I could and would literally walk down the hall, open a door, and I was in a public school hallway. As a result, I spent quite a bit of time in the middle school and became friends with many of the teachers. The FI was the perfect place for someone like me. It allowed me to stay connected with classroom practice every day.

The official mission of the FI was to promote the use of technology in schools in order to prepare North Carolina students for work and life in the 21st century. Because of that, there was a massive amount of reliance on and reverence paid to what I call "technology for technology's sake." Over the first few years at the FI, I had the chance to develop and deliver training on the classroom uses of digital lab equipment, video production, photography, laptop computers, GPS systems, interactive whiteboards, and more.

I was always skeptical about the classroom implementation of these technologies and some of the other work I was asked to do. It was as if some of the professors who directed grants and projects at the FI were not necessarily focused on solving problems with practical solutions. Instead, it seemed like the goal might have been to convince a company or organization to give money to the FI in order to design how a specific tool or device could be used in the classroom. This resulted in a "technology frenzy," where many of the conversations at the FI were focused on using the newest technologies in classrooms, many times ignoring whether or not a technology was remotely practical or even addressed a specific problem.

Of course, my skepticism was likely grounded in the fact that this "technology as a solution" mentality was counter to my proposed solution, that we need more music in the classroom. And it baffled me that these technologies were so expensive and that the implementation of them in the classroom took more time and energy than many traditional strategies that achieved the same goals.

For example, many project leaders at the FI were over-the-moon excited about 1-to-1 initiatives. This means that every student will have a laptop in the classroom every day. People went nuts for this idea. School leaders lobbied for millions of dollars to get these devices. Staff members were hired to keep the computers running. Teachers would go through a few hours of training on how to use them, and off they would race into the future of education. Or, so it seemed.

Oftentimes, the laptops did not solve any problem that the teachers were having. Instead, they were forced to use these devices in their classrooms because the school leadership allocated the money to purchase them, and the school's reputation rested on the use of technology.

The reality of the situation was not very futuristic. Many teachers I observed in these 1-to-1 schools didn't allow the students to use the computers for two reasons. First, there were always major technical problems when 30 students used the laptops at once. There were bound to be at least three computers that would not be working properly, thus the teacher would burn instructional time trying to troubleshoot.

Second, the laptop distracted students from the learning goal. Teachers in these 1-to-1 schools would be trying their best to find a use for the computers in day-to-day activities. For example, it was common for the students to use the computers to write a paper. The students would frequently get off task and surf the internet while the teacher is running around troubleshooting technology issues. With not much learning happening, this ends up being an expensive and ineffective method for accomplishing the learning goal. A few pieces of paper and a pen would work much better.

Of course, there were a few teachers who were using the computers in innovative ways that seemed to promote student learning, but these were the exceptions not the rule.

A technology I worked closely with, as part of a grant, was the interactive whiteboard, a projected computer image on a whiteboard that is also a touch screen. Many people found the technology revolutionary because we could get students to come up to the front of the room and interact with the whiteboard during a lecture. They would say things like, "This will really engage students in classrooms." I didn't know what classrooms they were referring to when describing this as student engagement, but I used to have a student or two come to the front of the room during my lectures to write on the board, with markers or chalk, and it didn't seem that engaging (certainly not compared to students interacting with music).

An interactive whiteboard seemed to be a tool that attempted to increase the value of lecture. However, the downside was that it required teachers to learn a new technology and software to *possibly* achieve these benefits. So many technologies were similar to these whiteboards. Most took too much time to implement for some unknown benefit.

Almost every teacher I worked with around this time was running a lecture-based classroom. I was able to identify with this pedagogy because it was exactly what I had done in my classroom. Thus, I always tried to put these new technologies through my filter of *would I use this in my classroom?* Most of the time the answer was "Absolutely not." The reason was because many of the new technologies made teaching more difficult. Yes, maybe the result *looks* better or maybe it's *slightly* more effective, but if everyone is just trying to get through their content, there is not a lot of time to integrate new practices. When I was teaching, I would break the rules, veer from the pacing guide to try a music-based lesson and then have to catch up. It didn't seem fair to ask teachers to do the same in order to use a tool that they may not be passionate about.

However, I continued to design strategies and deliver professional development or training in spite of it seeming to do little or nothing to help solve real problems for teachers. Many times, teachers I worked with would give feedback about my training saying, "Yeah, that technology is really cool, but I don't have time to use that in my classroom." I totally understood that. There was barely time to use the restroom between classes, let alone try to figure out how to use laptops or an interactive whiteboard to improve student learning.

CHAPTER 9
Music-Based Teaching

• • •

ENOUGH ABOUT OTHER PEOPLE'S AGENDAS, let's get back to mine. While continuing to explore the myriad of technology solutions promoted by the FI, I started working on my dissertation. A dissertation is like a really boring book that nobody would ever buy. My good friend Dr. Kenny once said, "The number of people who will read any given dissertation is three, plus or minus two, and your mother does not count." Even though he was joking, it's not far from the reality. When writing a dissertation, you are required to "elevate your language into the academic realm." To me that meant that I was required to adopt a particular writing style in an attempt to sound smarter than 99 percent of the people in the world. In turn, only my peers can read my work, but they won't want to because they believe their ideas are far superior to mine (and they're busy writing their own papers). If for some reason they do read my work, it will be so they can criticize and tear down my ideas. In fact, they have a name for this type of aggressive interaction. It's called "academic discourse."

When I finished my dissertation, I was required to defend it, willingly opening myself up to this academic discourse for about an hour while my advisors and committee members grilled me with questions about my research. The defense is the last in a series of hoops that one must jump through to complete a Ph.D. program. If you navigate all of them, you pop out the other side a little worse for wear, but for the rest of your life you can force people to call you "doctor," followed by saying, "I'm not that kind of doctor." Believe you me, it never gets old.

My dissertation was a chance for me to look scientifically and closely at the impact of my music-based teaching process. I took this opportunity to discover why my teaching methods worked so well in the classroom. It gave me an opportunity to write a 100+ page document that I can hold up in someone's face who doubted my teaching abilities and say, "See here. I did the right things in the classroom. Here is research and data that prove I was a great teacher. By the way, if you don't use music-based teaching, then you are doing it wrong." I know that sounds a bit petty, but that's how insecure I was at the time. I needed a document to feel validated.

The title of my dissertation was "Chemistry to Music: How Music-Based Teaching Affects Academic Achievement and Motivation in an 8th Grade Science Class."[6] I know I didn't sell it very well earlier, but you can be one of my "plus twos" if you would like. Most of you won't read it (I don't blame you), so here's a quick overview in non-academic jargon (i.e., regular language).

CHEMISTRY TO MUSIC

I wrote a series of songs about eighth grade chemistry and had Ms. C, a middle school teacher, use the songs as the basis for her instruction in two of her four science classes. In the other two classes, she did traditional lecture-based instruction. The treatment classes (where the music was used) had only a few adjustments. First, she would play the song and have students read the lyrics multiple times during each lesson. She would do this to focus students on the content. Instead of giving an assessment at the beginning of the class period (this is what she did in her control classes, the ones not using the music), she would simply play the song.

Then, instead of giving a traditional lecture (which she gave in her control classes), she would go through the lyrics of the song and explain what each line meant. Simply put, instead of using her typical lecture

---

6 Chemistry to Music. Retrieved from http://schooled.lodgemccammon.com

material, she lectured on the content by explicating the lyrics. It's important to note that Ms. C spent the same amount of time teaching the content to the music-based treatment classes as the traditional control classes.

Here is a sample of the lyrics and explanation from the first song used in this science class. It's called "We are Matter."[7] The lyrics are bold and the lecture notes are under each lyric.

Matter is anything that takes up space
NOTES: Matter – anything that has mass and takes up space

That has a mass or a volume, like a guitar case
PROBLEM: Have a picture of a guitar case that weighs 25lbs. How many kg of mass does it have? [25lbs/2.2lbs=11.4kg] What is its volume if length=120cm, width=40cm, height=10cm. Make sure to express the units. 120cm x 40cm x 10cm = 48000cm3
CALCULATE: Convert to cubic meters [48m3]

So measure matter matter – yeah matter
In a number of ways
NOTES: The ways to measure matter – mass (kg), volume (L), or (cm3), Density (mass/volume) g/L or g/cm3

We are matter, yeah we take up space
QUESTION: Why are we matter – pull from definition? [Because we have mass and take up space] What are things that exist that are not matter? [thoughts, feelings, websites?]

Whether kilograms or liters we displaced
Oh Kelly, Kelly what units - will you indicate
Cubic centimeters sound so great

---

7 Curriculum Music. Retrieved from http://schooled.lodgemccammon.com

QUESTION: Of all the ways to measure matter, is cubic centimeters the best way for measuring "our" matter? Why or why not? [It is not the best or most accurate way because we are an irregular object.] What might be other/better ways of measuring "our" matter? Why are they better? [Water displacement would be a better way of measuring volume because it is more accurate for irregular objects]

I found that academic achievement remained close to the same between the two groups (treatment and control), but motivation for learning increased in the classes where the music-based teaching was used. We also know from research that if we can increase student motivation for learning, it can eventually lead to increased achievement. Therefore, one of the conclusions was that music-based teaching could be used to increase student motivation for learning eighth grade science and eventually the increased motivation would result in increased student success.

I finally had some specific research and data to back up my agenda, quell my insecurities, and reinforce my ego. Now, I could finally say that, "I used music in the classroom and my students liked it because they were more motivated to learn. You should use it too because you will likely get the same results." This was a great finding because one common issue that I heard many teachers talk about was a lack of student motivation. There seemed to be a growing concern about how to motivate students who are so engaged by or addicted to technology outside the classroom. Music-based teaching seemed to create a better, more engaging classroom experience for most students.

This study also showed how a music-based lesson could take the same amount of time to implement as the lecture-based lesson (instead of taking more time, as was my initial experience). It was important that Ms. C could increase student motivation using music and lyrics without taking up additional class time or sacrificing time spent on other content.

CHAPTER 10

The Reinforcement of a Little Fame

• • •

RIGHT AROUND THE TIME I was working on this music-based teaching study for my dissertation, I had three important and groovy music-related things happen, all in 2007.

FIRST

As I explored the use of music in the classroom with Ms. C in early 2007, we stumbled onto something fascinating and important. We had already collected the data for my study, but the students responded so favorably to the music-based teaching treatment that we decided to keep working together. A number of students who did not get to participate in the original music-based teaching treatment expressed interest in using the songs in class because they had heard that it was fun. This meant that I would write more songs about eighth grade science and she would keep using them with all her classes, not just the original two from the study.

One evening I was having dinner with Ms. C at a local Mexican restaurant, and we were talking about how to make the music-based teaching even more powerful. I had previously taught with her at Wakefield High School, so she knew that I used to bring in my portable audio recorder to school and have the students sing the curriculum songs that I wrote for my classes. She also knew that I would video record them while they were singing, and share the music videos on the morning announcements. She thought both of those ideas were interesting, but did not think that they would work for her classroom. You see, Ms. C was not a singer, so she did not feel comfortable leading the students in that activity. She also didn't have a recording device to capture the singing, nor did she know how to use that type of equipment. Additionally, she did not know how to edit video and didn't want to take the time to learn. So, we decided those technologies were not practical.

Over tacos (with guacamole – I know it costs extra) I asked her in more detail about how the students were responding to the music. Now, keep in mind that I felt it important to mostly stay out of her classroom while she was implementing these music-based teaching strategies. I observed a few times, but that was it. Me *not* participating would make for a better story when trying to convince other teachers about the practicality of my music-based teaching method. It would be impractical if I had simply brought in my recording studio and cameras, recorded the students, edited the video and brought in the completed product just like I had done in my classroom at Wakefield. That would mean the only way another teacher could use the strategies was if they purchased the expensive equipment and developed my skillset.

Throughout dinner, as Ms. C was talking more about how the students would react to the songs, something jumped out at me. She said that as the students became familiar with the songs, after listening a few times, many would tend to get out of their seats and start moving around while the song was playing. She referred to this as "dancing." Well, that seemed interesting. Students dancing around the classroom while listening to a song about chemistry seemed like the poster child of what classroom engagement should look like, right? They would be learning through movement. How awesome is that?

Earlier that day I had borrowed something called a Flip camera from the technology department at the FI and had it with me at dinner. It was a pocket-sized video camera. I removed it from my pocket and said, "What if you challenged the students to create interpretive dances or movements that illustrate their understanding of the content, set up this little camera, and then recorded them performing their movements in one continuous take while the music is playing in the classroom?"

I went on to explain that after the video was recorded on the camera, it could be viewed immediately, and the students would be able to instantly see their work. This would not require her to do any video editing, it would not require her or the students to sing, and it could easily document their excitement for the content. All she needed was one $80 Flip camera. I lent her mine, so she could try that lesson the following day.

Ms. C did just that. Her classes were studying changes in states of matter and were using a song I wrote called "Someday Sublimate."[8] She gave the students time to work on moves that corresponded with the lyrics. Then she put them all in the back of the room, played the song and had the students do their moves. I was not in the classroom to see this lesson plan unfold firsthand, however, she showed me the video of the students' performance. The result was a complete nightmare (bet you thought I was going to say it was a success). It was utter chaos complete with 25 students jumping and gyrating all over the place. "Do not show it to anyone else," I told her. It looked like the exact opposite of classroom management. It looked as if the students were goofing around, and no teacher wanted anyone to think that students goof around in their classroom. We needed to modify the approach.

Finding a silver lining, we agreed that the students were certainly engaged in the activity, but needed a lot more structure. We made three very simple tweaks. First, students would need to be put into groups and each

8 Science Songs. Retrieved from http://schooled.lodgemccammon.com

group would be assigned to work on a small part of the song. Second, students would be required to explain how their movements corresponded to the content (to minimize the random jumping and gyrating). And third, their participation and explanations would be graded.

She tried the lesson the following day with these tweaks and voila, it worked great! Like so many lesson plans, the devil is in the details. There is such a fine line between chaos and success in the classroom. In fact, this experience with Ms. C and later experiences I had with teachers using music taught me that every innovation or new idea that is implemented in a classroom passes through two filters.

First, it must pass through the "relationships" filter. If the students don't care about or respect the teacher, it is likely that any innovation or new idea will fail because the students will simply refuse to buy in, leading the teacher to conclude that this new strategy does not work in their classroom. Ms. C had great relationships with her students and did not have a problem with this filter. Second, it passes through the "structure" filter. Like in the example above, we had not established the proper procedures that would allow the music-based lesson to be successful. Once we made the adjustments and she established the appropriate structure, the lesson was highly effective.

Why are these filters important? Well, they make it difficult for anyone to claim that a new idea *will* work in the classroom. All we can really say is that a new idea *can* work, if the students believe in the teacher and if the lesson is properly structured. In fact, almost any new strategy *can* work if these two filters are functioning properly.

After adjusting the second filter in Ms. C's classroom, the whole music-based teaching process was powerful. Allowing students to get up and move seemed to drastically increase excitement for learning. Assigning small student groups to come up with movements that illustrated the information in the song was challenging and fostered student collaboration. Some students were understandably reluctant to "dance," but most were over-the-top enthusiastic about the opportunity to express their learning in this active and alternative way. It was as if they were finally allowed to be children in school. Let's not forget that eighth grade students are still kids. Allowing the students to express themselves physically seemed like a big win for classroom engagement. Ms. C used this strategy with every song from that point on.

Ms. C really enjoyed using music-based teaching enhanced by these music videos. She also continued to report that the students were enthusiastic about getting up and moving to create and perform. Additionally, she started to tell me that the students were extremely interested and excited to watch these videos back. She found that students would want to watch these simple music videos over and over during class time and would even ask for copies to share with friends and family. Ms. C found ways of sharing the videos, according to the rules of her school, so that students could revisit their creations outside the classroom.

While Ms. C was regularly using music-based learning in her classroom, we quickly discovered a kink. The lessons where she allowed students to create, perform and review music videos were taking a lot longer than her traditional lessons. She saw great value in the teaching method but was simply not able to keep up with her pacing guide. As a result, she had to do the same thing I did when I was in the classroom. She would have days when she was forced to cover a massive amount of material in a very traditional way to catch up. Like me, she was able to make it work, but it always came at a cost. Keep that in mind.

SECOND

Later in 2007, Steve Dembo, an education guru who worked for Discovery Education, contacted me about my curriculum songs after seeing a music video featuring a group of North Carolina administrators. These school leaders had created an interpretive dance to a song that I had written about cells, so I filmed them performing it using the one-take recording technique that I had developed with Ms. C. Someone sent Steve that video and he visited my website to learn more about my education music. After listening to a few songs, he called me and asked if I would be interested in licensing my songs to Discovery Education. Doing so would mean that the songs would be distributed to classrooms across the world in their service called Discovery Education *Streaming*. I told him, "Yes, I am absolutely interested!" This further supported my theory that music must be the answer. More proof.

Discovery Education is the education arm of Discovery Communications (think Discovery Channel, Animal Planet, etc.) and they want to distribute my education songs in a service that is purchased by over 50 percent of the schools in the United States, and many more worldwide. This was a huge deal for quelling my insecurity and stoked the heck out of my ego. A few months later, my songs were available to millions of teachers and students for use inside and outside of the classroom.

In addition to licensing my songs, Discovery would frequently invite me to events around the country to talk about and demonstrate how I use music to enhance learning. Essentially, they handed me a national stage where I could speak about my solution, allowing me to develop what was described sometime later as a "cult following." There are a decent number of teachers around the world who are die-hard fans of my education songs, and I appreciate the heck out of every single one of them.

THIRD

Also in 2007 (it was a big year for me), I collaborated with two colleagues, Brian Bouterse and Sammie Carter, who worked for the technology group at the FI to create an entry for an online video contest. A company called

VMware – they make server virtualization software – launched the contest. We heard about the contest because Sammy and Brian were on a VMware email list and got a message about it three days before the submissions were due. To enter the video contest, we had to create a two-minute-or-less video explaining how we use VMware at work and why it's great. Seemed easy enough. Sammie and Brian knew the answers to those two questions because they were VMware experts, and I had some ideas on what type of video we could make.

I sat down with Brian and asked him about how we used VMware at the FI and why it was great. He talked for about 15 minutes while I took notes. Then, I found Sammie and asked him the same questions. He talked for about 20 minutes while I took notes. After learning all about VMware from the fellas, I took that information and wrote a 1:51 song called "Virtualized Hardware Hotel."[9] For me, this process was similar to creating an education song; the content was a little different, but I still used music and lyrics to express complex concepts. Below is a sample of the lyrics and explanation.

(Verse 1 Lyrics)
We use VMware to automate the creation of servers
A hundred images in a matter of minutes
Without configuring 100 separate machines
We can rapidly create and destroy among chaos and riots
And use a bunch of thin, thin clients
With no phone calls interrupting my dreams

(Verse 1 Explanation)
The software essentially allows you to transform hardware into software. On a single large server, you can create a number of virtual computers and allow them to share hardware resources without interfering with each other. Each virtual machine has its own

---

9 Virtualized Hardware Hotel. Retrieved from http://schooled.lodgemccammon.com

processor, RAM, hard disk and network controller. And each can run an operating system and applications independently of the other virtual machines. Chaos happens when you have one IT person trying to service hundreds of computer users. With a centralized server running hundreds of virtual machines, it's easier to solve problems quickly. Thin clients are lightweight, low-energy computers people use to access the virtual machines. Let's say you have an older computer with a slow processor, a small amount of RAM and no software applications other than your operating system. That would also be a thin client. If you logged on to a Friday Institute virtual machine, you could run programs on your computer as if you had a fast processor, a ton of RAM and the most current applications.

After the music and lyrics were done, we filmed a video. This was the final day to submit to the contest, so we needed to be quick about it. Since we had extremely limited time, the video consisted of only three clips. It opens with Sammie sitting at a meeting table saying, "So, tell me about VMware." The second clip is Brian walking through the hallways of the FI to the server room, lip-syncing the lyrics in time with the song. The third and final clip is Sammie making a pithy joke on the refrain of the song. He says, "So, what if the servers go down?" Within the course of about an hour, we set up, practiced and recorded those three video clips. Then, I edited them together, adding the music track during Brian's walk.

After watching the completed video and having a good laugh, we uploaded it to the contest website minutes before the deadline, then went to grab beer and laugh some more about our creation. The video quality was certainly not perfect or professional. I put a camera on top of a cardboard box that was sitting on a rolling cart to film Brian's lip sync walk around the building, so the video was pretty shaky and had an amateur look to it. Regardless of the aesthetic shortcomings, our 1:59 submission was awesome because it was so real.

Due to the tight timeline for completion, we didn't have the option to re-record the video. Even though the video quality left something to be desired, the content was clear. It reminded me of the videos that Ms. C made in the classroom. They were not professionally recorded, but were simple and powerful.

Side note: It took me 35 minutes to learn the content and 90 minutes to write and record the song. It took about 60 minutes to practice and film the clips. It took another 60 minutes to edit the three video clips together, add the song, render, review, and publish the completed project. That seemed like a lot of work for such a simple video, but the three of us had fun and were very happy with the result.

About two weeks later I received a call from someone at VMware informing me that our video had been selected as the winner of the VMware Virtually Famous contest. WHAT?! The prize was $15,000. I was handed another data point to validate why music is a powerful force and absolutely the solution to the problems in education. I created a curriculum song (information about VMware) and it was worth $15,000 to a corporation. Wow, first Discovery Education and now this? I was beyond excited!

Because we won the contest, the three of us were flown out to San Francisco to be recognized at VMware's yearly conference called VMworld.[10] They announced our video as the winner in front of 10,000 people and brought us up on stage where we shook hands with people in suits and received the $15,000 check. It was surreal, but that was not the end of it.

Throughout the day, Brian and Sammie were constantly recognized by conference attendees as being "those guys in the music video" (not me because I was not in the video). The video had made them celebrities.

---

10 VMworld Experience – I like to document things. Retrieved from http://schooled.lodgemccammon.com

That evening, we were invited to attend an extravagant party on Treasure Island, off the coast of San Francisco. VMware bussed over the 10,000 conference attendees to a section of the island where they had rented and decorated a huge airplane hangar.

This celebration offered unlimited food, drink and entertainment (music, magicians, fire-breathers) throughout the evening. Because we won the contest, we were given VIP passes that allowed us to hang out in a private section of the venue where the important people (CEO, vice presidents, etc.) were spending their time. This also gave us access to go behind the main music stage and hang out with Smash Mouth, the head-lining band.

It was as if we were "Walkin' on the Sun" (a Smash Mouth hit from the late 90s). We walked into a tent where the band was standing around taking pictures with all the VIPs. When it was my turn to get a picture, I walked right up to the lead singer, Steve Harwell, and said, "Man, I am a huge fan. I really dig your work." He looked at me and said, "Thanks, man!" and shook my hand. Then, I blurted out in the most uncool way possible, "We won a video contest." He just said, "Ah. Ok. Cool." We hung around their tent for a while until they went out to play. All in all, it was quite a night.

Everything seemed to be coming up Millhouse (Simpsons reference). The music endeavors were going great. I had this warm core inside my teacher-y soul that was burning bright because I believed that I had actually solved the problem in education. I was ready to say that the reason why classrooms are not awesome is because not enough of them are using the incredible power of music, enhanced by allowing students to physically demonstrate the content. I think I even changed my Facebook status at this point to highlight the famous Emma Goldman quote, "A revolution without dancing is not a revolution worth having." Now that I knew music was the solution, it was time to make a battle plan for how to convince everyone else.

THE STERLING PRINCIPLE

One evening I was hanging out with a group of friends, many of whom were teachers. I was likely sharing with them all the recent success with my music career. Basically, I was both bragging and offering unsolicited advice on how to be a better teacher and I could hardly hear myself talk over the sound of the collective eye rolling. In the moment, I wrote it off that they were jealous and did not have any solutions of their own. They had not put in the time to figure out what I had figured out, so of course they are going to be jealous. Also, they were all probably stuck thinking that what *they* were currently doing in *their* classrooms was the gold standard, and that the way they were currently teaching was their superhero power. But I just kept talking despite them not being overly attentive or receptive to my ideas. Suddenly, my friend Sterling (one of the teachers who I was talking at – yes, at) asked a question that made my music-based teaching house of cards come tumbling down. He asked, "Do you have songs that I can use in my psychology class?"

Just like that, it became crystal clear that music-based teaching, in the way that I was touting it, could not be the solution unless there were songs for every topic that students learn about in school. There would need to be thousands of curriculum songs, and I had only created 30 over the past two years. It would take me many lifetimes to even scratch the surface on creating songs for all classrooms. Just like that, I was back at square one.

Sterling was exactly right. In order to have a real solution to a broad problem, the solution needs to apply to every teacher at every level and content area. That is a much bigger challenge than what I had been working on for the past few years. I needed to take a more macro approach to the problem. I needed to look at teachers in the aggregate. I needed to look at thousands of classrooms, not just teachers who were willing to use the materials that I developed. Yet again, I realized that it was not about me. The solution is not my personality and not my music.

CHAPTER 11

$15,000

• • •

You might be wondering about the contest money I won from VMware. Did we divide it up three ways? Did I take it all and buy something nice like a fancy shed? None of the above. It turns out that our winning video was worth way more than the $15,000 prize money. It was a wakeup call for me along my quest.

How was it even possible that an amateur-looking video won such a big prize? It was because sites like YouTube, which allow everyone to broadcast any style or quality of video, were becoming extremely popular and changing the aesthetic of what was visually palatable. Simply put, we as a viewing society had seen, created and shared so many "low quality" videos that nobody seemed to care how things looked. If a friend sends me a video of her cat dancing to a techno song, I don't care about the video quality. I just want to see that crazy cat dancing. It was much more important for the content to be strong than the video to look good.

I found it fascinating that as technology raced forward, allowing professional video creators access to tools unlike any time in history to create flawless HD quality video, the video filmed with an $80 Flip camera was on equal footing as something created in a million dollar TV studio. What an exciting world.

Since technically I won the contest (my song, video, concept and name on the submission), it was my choice what to do with the cash. I decided to donate it to the FI (where I had just been hired full time to do professional development) and use it as seed funding for a new project, called FIZZ, that was all about exploring the classroom applications of what I called "one-take video."[11]

Using any type of video camera, any teacher can create a one-take video by hitting record on their camera or cell phone, filming something of educational value (like a student-created music video about matter), and hitting stop. The product is then completely done. This low-barrier video technique can be used by any teacher or student to rapidly generate meaningful classroom content. In fact, most of the billions of videos on YouTube are one-take videos. The internet is loaded with one-take videos of dogs, cats, skateboarding, opinions, and so much more. I wanted to use this same popular strategy to enhance the learning environment.

With the money, I hired an undergraduate assistant, Luke, who was taking classes in the College of Education. We purchased a case of Flip cameras and software that we installed on the Friday Institute servers (running VMware, of course), which would act as private YouTube sites. This allowed us to create independent video sharing websites that we called FIZZ sites.

The idea of creating video in classrooms was fairly novel back in 2007, and the main concern for many teachers and education leaders was safety. It was important to guard against student work and images being uploaded to unseemly public spaces like YouTube. To solve this issue, we created private video sharing sites for each FIZZ partner school or classroom, so that the content available on the site could be completely controlled.

---

11 One-Take Video. Retrieved from http://schooled.lodgemccammon.com

We traveled around North Carolina giving out Flip cameras and of-fering these private YouTube sites to schools across the state. We trained hundreds of educators on how to use Flip cameras in concert with the FIZZ sites, but we were also interested in exploring what one-take strategies were practical for classrooms. More specifically, we knew it was important to teach educators more than just how to use the tools, we wanted to teach them specific ways of using video to create active learning environments.

After traveling around the state for a few months, working with teach-ers and students, I developed a few Sterling-approved (meaning every teacher could use them because they were content and grade level ag-nostic) one-take video strategies for the classroom. Each of the following strategies emphasize the idea that video quality and aesthetic was much less important than the clarity of the content.

Strategy #1: Video Scavenger Hunt.[12] Teachers review their content and identify a handful of concepts that students can either find around the school or that they can physically demonstrate (e.g., right angles, evapora-tion). The teacher puts students into groups, gives them a list of topics, hands them a camera and challenges them to make a short one-take video about each topic. Once all the groups are done, the videos are viewed and discussed to reinforce the content. This is an active and fun lesson plan that can be used in any classroom.

Strategy #2: Lesson Openers.[13] Teachers or students create a one-take video somewhere in the real world that brings a concept to life, and then they play it back in the classroom. For example, a teacher creates a one-take lesson opener video about photosynthesis while walking around a local lake, referencing the different types of plants. Or a student might create one on how to calculate price per ounce in the grocery store. The basic idea is for the teacher or student to always be on the lookout

---

12 Right Angles One-take Scavenger Hunt.
13 Photosynthesis One-take Lesson Opener.
Retrieved from http://schooled.lodgemccammon.com

for ways of connecting classroom learning to the real world, using the simple one-take video strategy to bring that context into the classroom to reinforce the learning.

Strategy #3: Paperslide Videos.[14] They are as simple as they sound. Teachers or students write a script about a topic and create images on pieces of paper that correspond with what they wrote. Then, they point a video camera down at a flat surface, hit record, read the script while sliding in the images, hit stop, and their one-take paperslide video is complete. This is a low-barrier way to promote student collaboration and creation.

One-take paperslide videos were immediately popular because the strategy was easy to understand and something that teachers could use to challenge students to teach the content. Teachers found that the paperslide artifacts of learning, including student voice and images, helped to quickly uncover student misconceptions. There was no way to "fake" an understanding if students were recording a video. Many students were inspired to create the best products possible because they were motivated by the fact that the videos would be played for, reflected on and discussed by the entire class. Additionally, students were motivated because their product might be selected by the teacher to be published online as a representation of learning. This was a much more engaging lesson plan than, for example, having students work collaboratively on a worksheet.

The paperslide strategy was powerful because teachers could start to leverage the benefits of peer teaching. When students were working in groups to create the script and images, they were teaching each other. When the students were practicing and recording their paperslide presentation, they were teaching each other. And when the class was watching the paperslide videos and discussing them, again, they were teaching each other. In my experience, this type of peer teaching can have a positive

---

14 Paperslide Videos. Retrieved from http://schooled.lodgemccammon.com

impact on student achievement (if the two filters are working), not to mention that repetition of information certainly doesn't hurt.

RECORD

Since I was heavily promoting the use of the one-take video strategy, it seemed appropriate that I should use it as much as possible. I encouraged teachers to either be on the lookout for recordable moments outside the classroom or design recordable moments in the classroom to better engage students. I wanted every teacher and student to walk around with a video camera in his or her pocket, ready to capture learning anywhere. So, that's exactly what I did. I recorded hundreds of videos over the next year or so.[15]

I carried a Flip camera with me at all times. If I saw that a sink had a great design, I would record a one-take video about it and post it to Facebook. If I saw a strange bug, I would record and share it. If I found that kicking my air conditioner made it work again, I would record and share. If I found a wig in the middle of a parking lot while on a trip, I would record and share it. In addition to the one-take videos I was creating with teachers and students across North Carolina, I was also creating a ton of "other" content. I was training myself to integrate the one-take video recording and publishing process into my everyday life.

At the beginning of this journey, recording and publishing a single video was, initially, a huge deal. Editing those music videos for my classes at Wakefield High School took lots of planning, time and effort. However, after years of recording and publishing literally thousands of videos, creation has become as natural as breathing because I made the process simple with the one-take mindset. Now, I just want teachers and students to feel the same way I do. I want them to create, record, publish and reflect every day.

---

15 Greatest Fits, a selection of random one-take videos. Retrieved from http://schooled.lodgemccammon.com

Professional Development

I learned a lot in 2008 traveling around North Carolina promoting one-take video strategies during school or district professional development days. In the very first session, I used a traditional teaching method to deliver the content. I stood up in front of 35 high school teachers in the media center and delivered the information to them while they were sitting down. I lectured about how one-take videos worked and outlined the benefits. I talked about how each strategy could be used in the classroom. I showed student and teacher-created samples. I talked through the details of using the Flip cameras and FIZZ sites.

I had become the professor in front of the room, telling (probably arrogantly) these teachers what they "needed" to know. I had my PowerPoint. The audience was sitting quietly, passively listening to what I was saying. Some were grading while I was talking because the use of one-take video in the classroom was not a requirement in their school, just another thing they could opt to do if they had some free time. I did not blame them for not being engaged. I did not blame them for ignoring me while I talked. I knew that most of them, like me, when I was a high school teacher, didn't have time for anything extra.

A few days after this session, I checked the FIZZ site that we set up for the teachers who attended the training and realized that they were not using it at all. This probably also meant that they were not using the one-take video strategies either. While it was disappointing, it made sense. Many of the teachers were not engaged in my lecture. Shocked? Me either.

I had shared simple tools and strategies for enhancing their classrooms. Yet, there was basically zero evidence that anyone was actually doing it. I had spent time and energy traveling to the school, preparing my lecture, assembling examples and talking about what I had created, but I saw no results. Even though the responses on the session evaluation were great (almost all 35 said that they really enjoyed the session), I decided that something needed to change. Just like in the classroom, when I did not get a desired outcome from the students, I needed to rethink the way I was teaching the content. So, I decided to try a different approach.

Empathy helped me to craft a new professional development strategy. I thought back through some of the professional development sessions I sat through and those that I had provided over the years. There was a strong possibility that the teachers in those sessions were extremely tired from teaching and not able to connect with what I was saying. I had to also assume that each teacher in the room had their own agenda, and they considered themselves to be a superhero. Thus, they might not be interested in listening to new ideas.

If I assume all those things about any group of teachers in a professional development session, I can assume they are a very difficult audience. I knew from personal experience that lecture was not a great way to deliver information to a difficult audience. Most of the professional development I received as a teacher was done through lecture, and it was largely ineffective in terms of resulting in any type of change to my classroom.

I decided that instead of lecture, I needed to model my new strategies and allow the teachers (my students for the day) to have time to experiment with both the strategies and tools, in order for the session to be a useful experience. I needed them to get actively involved in the presentation. They needed to be out of their seats and collaborating, experiencing what their students would experience if they used these strategies. If I am just lecturing to them, that gives the teachers the ability to just pretend to pay attention. If they are engaged with the content, it would be much harder to tune me out.

This fit in with my larger understanding of good education. Back when I was teaching, I was convinced that the days when I engaged students with active learning were the most beneficial. Thus, I wanted to follow the same guidelines with these professional development sessions that I was leading. Luckily, I had the flexibility to do this because my training sessions did not have a pacing guide, so I would be able to cut out some of the lecture content to make room for participant engagement.

During the next few sessions, instead of lecturing on the strategies, I modeled the use of the strategies. I pretended that I was a teacher in a science class and that the participants were my students. I had them experience what it was like to be a student and participate in a lesson that used one-take video. They made one-take videos about sublimation, and then uploaded them to the FIZZ sites. After we learned by doing, I encouraged them to ask questions about anything that was unclear. After answering questions, I gave the teachers time to collaborate and decide how they could use the strategies in their unique classrooms. Then, I asked them to design a lesson using each strategy and present their idea to the larger group. If nothing else, teachers were out of their seats, working together, creating, laughing and sharing ideas. Teachers were not able to sit and grade during these sessions. I was having them work.

Getting participants actively involved in the session, using what I referred to as modeling-based professional development, resulted in better outcomes, whether increasing understanding of the content or actively using the strategies. After the sessions where I used modeling, higher quality artifacts of teaching and learning were showing up on the FIZZ sites. It seemed as easy as that. If I wanted educators to use new strategies and tools, I had to go beyond lecturing. I needed to model how they could be used in a classroom.[16]

Modeling proves to a group of teachers that I am their peer. It allows me to gain their trust. Teachers don't usually get to watch other teachers teach. When they do, I have found them to be extremely judgmental,

---

16 Modeling-Based Professional Development. Retrieved from
http://schooled.lodgemccammon.com

citing their own agenda as the gold standard and then using that standard to explain how the teacher they are observing is doing it wrong. Many times, they won't give critical feedback. Instead, they will say things like, "What that teacher is doing would never work in my classroom."

The challenge for providing effective professional development is to present new ideas while also modeling excellent pedagogy so that teachers will hopefully look at what I am doing and remark, "Wow, he is a good teacher. I want to be more like him." It's a simple concept, but tough to successfully execute because you have to actually be a good teacher. There is no way to fake that.

Additionally, my modeling works well because it requires collaboration. I built in time for the teachers to talk to each other about what they were experiencing. Allowing teachers a few minutes after each modeled lesson to chat with a peer and process the information can be critical for buy-in. It gives the participants a chance to teach each other what they think was useful and important, instead of always hearing from the lecturer. It works the same way in the classroom. It's always good to allow students a chance to teach each other their version of the content.

In fact, this participant collaboration might be the best strategy for dealing with a difficult audience. Let's say that half the teachers in the room are willfully not interested in the content being presented during the professional development session I am leading (which is not unusual during a mandatory session). After I model a lesson, I can put them in groups to discuss. The hope would be that at least one teacher in every group would have been engaged by the strategy, and now it's their turn to repackage and pitch the merits of the content to their peers. This simple strategy takes some of the pressure off me as a presenter. I always know that the participants will be encouraged to interact with the content from a number of angles, not just me telling them what to think.

Teachers were generally more excited about my modeling-based professional development sessions. More people came up at the end and said thank you. More came up and exclaimed that the time went by very quickly because they were constantly doing activities. More teachers ended up using the strategies back in their classrooms.

Strangely, although most participants *said* they really liked it, the feedback on the session evaluations was actually worse than when I would just lecture about the content. When I would lecture during training sessions, the session evaluation feedback was consistent. Most teachers would write generic and positive responses like, "the session was good" or "the presenter did a fine job." This was because they were used to this delivery method. It's what they experience all the time. However, now I was changing it up. I was requiring them to get up and move. I was requiring them to think, collaborate and share. I was not allowing them to sit and do other work. While most teachers were over the moon excited about being active in their learning, a few in every group were downright angry. So, while my positive feedback remained extremely positive, my negative feedback was more extreme. I even had one teacher write in the session evaluation, "Stop wasting our time trying to engage us. Just tell us what we need to know and leave."

I found that this was very similar to what can happen in the classroom. Students have experienced so many passive (lecture-based) learning environments and have learned how to function in them, that being active is a shock to the system. It's like I was changing the game on these students. They had figured out the system. They pretend to pay attention. They do the minimum required. They leave. Well, not anymore. Change affects people differently. Some get angry.

Overall, my conclusion was that creating an active learning environment during professional development was not only more effective, but also most learners seemed to appreciate it. This is not surprising, but it's noteworthy because it was the first time I really thought of professional development sessions and training as just another classroom where the principles of what I considered to be good teaching resulted in benefits for learners.

DESPERATELY SEEKING ACTIVE LEARNING

I was ready at this point to reluctantly put a stake in the ground and guardedly start telling myself that I had uncovered the actual solution. The problem in education is that teachers are not using enough strategies to actively engage students. We know from decades of research that active learning environments, those where students are participating in the learning, promote academic achievement, as opposed to lecture-based passive learning environments. Therefore, my new agenda and solution, realizing that the answers were not hidden in a teacher's personality or the lyrics and music, was that every teacher should use one-take video strategies to get students involved in the learning. Also, I was convinced that active learning strategies should be used by professional development providers to create an engaging training experience. Active learning was not only the right thing for the classroom, but training teachers to use one-take video while modeling how it can create an active learning environment accelerated the spread of my new solution.

I thought about it like this: Starting out as a teacher, my hope was that the education system was going to shine a spotlight on me and say, "Look at Mr. McCammon. He is exactly the type of teacher we need. He cares so much that it inspires students to want to learn." Well, that didn't happen. Then, I was convinced that people were going to say, "Look at Dr. Lodge. He creates amazing songs that provide students with an incredible opportunity to learn content in a different way." That happened, but on a very small scale.

This next solution was less about me and what I do, and more about what others can do. To truly make a difference, I needed to start focusing on what the teachers were willing to do at the macro level, not on what only exceptional teachers could do.

CHAPTER 12

Algebra 1:
The End of an Era

• • •

HERE WE ARE IN THE summer of 2008. I successfully defended my dissertation and graduated with a Ph.D. from the College of Education at NC State with a focus on curriculum development. We are going to fast-forward a bit. Over the next two years, still working full time at the FI, I continued to learn more about the viability of music and one-take videos from the thousands of teachers across the country who I got to work with during my Discovery Education speaking engagements. The FIZZ project continued to expand as I offered more professional development sessions across North Carolina and the country, extolling the virtues of one-take videos.

It seemed like it was working. The more I modeled, the more teachers would use my ideas. I envisioned that the strategies would slowly expand and would take years to catch on. I enjoyed doing the work, so I was dedicated to spending years to allow the one-take video concept to be used in all classrooms.

In the meantime, I wanted to develop a product that combined everything that I had learned. I wanted to create a music-based curriculum enhanced with one-take video lessons for Algebra 1 teachers and students. Why Algebra 1? Well, in 2010, many schools were encouraging students to take Algebra 1 in eighth grade; it was previously taken by high school freshman. Therefore, many teachers and leaders were interested in checking out new ways to engage younger students in math classes.

Over the course of the next three months, I wrote and recorded a 13-song album covering Algebra 1 topics from the number system to exponential functions. I also created materials that went along with the songs. These materials included lyric explanations, worksheets and detailed lesson plans to guide teachers while they integrated the one-take strategies in the classroom.

The following is a sample lyric and explanation from one of my songs called "In Common"[17] about systems of equations. Notice, again, that I try to write song lyrics that require students to explicate and discuss instead of just memorizing. Reading the lyrics is meant to get students to say, "I wonder what that means" and challenge them to think in order to interpret.

Verse 3:
$y = x + 4$ and $y = 2x - 1$
We line up the variables
And multiply one equation ($-y = -2x + 1$)
So when we add the two equations
One variable goes, elimination
Then we solve for x
And use some substitution (5,9) is the solution

Explanation of Verse 3:
Verse 3 is taking us through how to find the solution for this system using elimination. First, we want to line up the two linear equations by their variables because we are going to add the two equations together.
$y = x + 4$
$y = 2x - 1$

---

17 Math Songs. Retrieved from http://schooled.lodgemccammon.com

Before we add them, we want to make sure that when we add them, that one of the variables cancels out - so that we are actually solving for the other variable. For example, we are going to multiply y = 2x - 1 by -1. This will make sure that the y becomes -y, therefore cancelling out when we add the two equations together. This will result in the following:

y = x + 4

-y = -2x + 1

The y variable cancels out and leaves us with x=5. Now, we want to take the x value (5) and substitute it back into one of the equations to solve for y. y = 5 + 4. y=9. The solution for this system is (5,9). This is where the two lines cross, and the coordinate that they share makes each equation true.

As I was developing these wicked-awesome songs and materials, I was also convincing myself that I was really designing a new method of teaching. This method of teaching was all about having that video camera ready to capture teacher and student work in a practical way, using the one-take methodology. This method could be enhanced by teachers having access to content songs; so not only could they create an active learning environment with the one-take video strategies, they could also use the music to increase motivation for learning.[18] I was able to cite myself now. This was exciting because one-take videos were something that every Algebra 1 teacher could and should use, and I had research to back it up.

It was time to start telling other teachers about what I had created. From my years of experience providing professional development, I knew that I needed to implement the modeling-based approach to get teachers to use the strategies and resources during the session. This meant that I would need to prepare sample lessons and activities where I would

---

18 McCammon, William GL, Jr. Chemistry to Music: How Music-Based Teaching Affects Academic Achievement and Student Motivation in an 8th Grade Science Class. Diss. North Carolina State U, 2008.

be teaching Algebra 1 to Algebra 1 teachers. This was an intimidating thought because, in my experience, math teachers were very passionate about their content (and were the ones who ripped down my "Ray says" signs in the bathrooms at Wakefield).

Not only did I have to prepare sample lessons, but I also needed to make sure that I was teaching them in such a way that they recognized and respected me as a fellow teacher, that they would be inspired by my teaching abilities (my superhero power). I believed that if I could convince them that I was a fellow math teacher, they would be inspired to integrate my Algebra 1 teaching methods and materials. So, off I went.

I facilitated a series of two-hour workshops for middle and high school Algebra 1 teachers around the state. I used my formula. During each workshop, I demonstrated the use of a one-take video lesson opener about the number system. We did a video scavenger hunt about the number system. We created a music video using my song about the number system. We recorded paperslide videos about the number system. We watched and discussed all the videos. Toward the end of the session, I shared a link to my website where they could find all the materials for the 13 lessons (including the one we used in the workshop) about Algebra 1, all for free. To finish the workshop, I had them get into groups and spend a few minutes talking about how they would use these lessons in their classrooms. Everything was going great right up until the end. Each group briefly shared what they had discussed regarding using my materials. I was both shocked and devastated at the feedback.

With only a few exceptions, groups either said that they would not be able to use these materials or that they might be able to play the song for their students as part of a warm up activity. That's it.

Now, I will say this. Almost every group was adamant that they really enjoyed the training. They said to my face and provided feedback on the session evaluation that they thought the training and materials were great. They said that they had a lot of fun creating one-take videos and collaborating with their peers throughout the workshop. Many also reported that they were convinced that the students would respond very well to these materials and this music-based teaching. The positive feedback was nice and all, but the overwhelming response was that the materials and one-take teaching strategies were not practical, realistic or helpful. How could this be? I needed to know why. So, I asked them.

Almost every group responded the same way. "I don't have time to use these materials and methods." Some even went so far as to say, "You don't remember what it's like in the classroom. We don't have time to get through our content as it is. We barely have time to go to the bathroom, so we certainly don't have time to integrate new ideas that will take up more class time."

Ugh. This was the same problem I had in my classroom. This is the same problem that Ms. C ran into when using the chemistry songs. It was the same problem that hundreds of teachers had been describing to me for years during the variety of professional development sessions I delivered. These teachers have pacing guides. They are responsible for getting students through all the information. Their principals probably say to them what Mr. Smith said to me when I was teaching at Wakefield High School: "Everyone needs to be doing everything they can to raise test scores. The best way to do this is by sticking to the pacing guide."

I had not forgotten about the problem of time, but I had been ignoring it. Suddenly I realized that the solution I had presented to them was not a solution at all. All I had basically said to them was that I had developed yet *another* thing for them to do. This "solution" I offered would take them off their pacing guide. After they spent time using my materials and method they would need to have those brutal lecture days to get caught up.

I had research to back up what I was "selling," but it made no difference. I had spent years developing materials and methods that were essentially useless from that macro perspective. I had become the professor in the room, down from the ivory tower, trying to push my agenda. The teachers were engaged during my modeling-based professional development and seemed to enjoy it, but that wasn't enough.

This took the air right out of my lungs. Over and over I heard, "I don't have time. I don't have time. I don't have time." So, to recap, it's not my personality, my content-based music, or one-take video strategies that can transform the classroom into a place of awesome active learning and amazing student engagement. It was clear at this point that I had been ignoring the actual problem. Back to the drawing board, then?

There are a ton of tools, strategies and teaching methods that can be used for creating active learning environments. A lack of resources is not the issue. All I had done was create more options. The real problem is that most teachers (in aggregate, at the macro level) don't have time to integrate any of those active teaching methods. It does not matter how cool the methods are. It does not matter how much research backs them up. It does not matter how you present them. If teachers don't have time to integrate new ideas, they are not going to integrate new ideas. Case closed.

I needed to figure out how to make time.

CHAPTER 13

Making Time

• • •

"STERLING'S PRINCIPLE" KEPT ME FOCUSED on the fact that I needed to create a solution to the problem of time that would be useful for all teachers. The solution could not be content or grade specific. The solution *definitely* could not be something that would take up more class time. Also, the popularity of the one-take paperslide video concept (many teachers were now using it with their students) suggested that any solution I created needed to be both easy to adopt and inexpensive.

I needed a fresh perspective to start solving this problem of time. I went back to my roots, what I did when I first decided I wanted to be a teacher, and spent a few months observing classrooms. I postponed my judgment regarding what I was seeing in these rooms. I was not there to judge the pedagogy or think about what I would do differently. I was there to answer one simple question: What are teachers doing with their class time? To solve the problem of time, I needed to understand how the time was being used.

Late in the fall of 2010, I observed a few classrooms in every grade level, kindergarten through graduate school (K-20). I visited all different types of schools (i.e., public, magnet, private, charter). And what I saw came as no surprise. Beyond third grade, the preponderance of instructional time was spent on lecture. Over and over I sat and watched teachers stand in the front of their rooms and cover the content while students sat passively, listening and learning.

To compliment these observations, I also interviewed administrators who ran many of these schools and asked them, on average, how much instructional time do teachers in their schools spend on lecture. Their feedback confirmed what I had seen. The average for elementary schools (after third grade) was 70 percent, middle school was 80 percent and high school was 90 percent or more.

It's likely that every one of the teachers I observed, like myself, had gone through a system of education where most of their personal experience of learning was sitting and listening to a teacher talk about the content. It makes all the sense in the world that they would replicate the techniques that they experienced throughout their entire lives. I certainly did.

I figured that time is the problem and based on the variety of classrooms I observed, most of the time is being spent on lecture. Thus, the lecture is what we need to zero in on. To be perfectly honest, since the first day of my teacher training up to that moment, I had heard education professors, teachers, trainers and leaders talk about getting rid of lecture. It struck me that they had found out long ago the same thing that I just found out. They realized that teachers spend most of their time lecturing to students, leaving little or no time to get students actively engaged in their learning. I never really paid much attention to those people who said, "We need to get rid of lecture." It had become a platitude of sorts; most of them just demonized the practice of lecturing without offering any practical alternative.

I recall a presentation I attended in the fall of 2010 where an author was speaking to a group of about 200 teachers. He was an advocate of arts integration. He wanted all teachers to buy his book and use his methods. That was his agenda. I remember clearly that not only was he saying lecture was a terrible strategy, but he went so far as to make fun of a teacher for defending the strategy. He regaled the audience with a story about a biology teacher who said, "I am not able to integrate the arts because I can't take the time away from covering the content." This teacher also mentioned that the arts integration strategies the author was promoting were too time consuming. The author, in retelling this story, said, "It's ridiculous that this biology teacher refused to simply abandon lecture in order to do the arts activities."

I want to point out that the author's entire presentation was a 60-minute lecture with PowerPoint. I found it a little ironic that he was demonizing lecture while lecturing. I realized that I had seen this a lot. In fact, everyone I ever met who talked about how terrible lecture was said it via lecture. It reminded me of my first few classes in my Ph.D. program when I realized that professors who were lecturing may not have the answers to creating engaging classrooms. If they did, they might not be lecturing the whole time.

Still, humans have been imparting knowledge through lecture for thousands of years. Simply telling a teacher to stop lecturing is not a solution. It doesn't work. Lecturing has a very specific function. It allows teachers to get through the content and stay with the pacing guide while controlling a classroom full of students. If we want teachers to stop using most of their class time lecturing, we need to provide a solution that achieves the same function.

Economic Reasoning

This problem of time allowed me to harken back to my undergraduate study of economics. In an economy, if the workforce is not producing the desired goods or services in an appropriate amount time, we need to improve efficiency. It's simple. Efficiency is all about using our limited resources in more productive ways. The most notable worldwide increase in efficiency over the past century has been due to the creation and use of technology. Many industries have been able to use their resources in smarter and better ways to produce more goods and services for the people of the world because of the many incredible high-tech inventions like robotic assembly lines or computers that facilitate instant global communication. The education industry needed a similar revolution. The workforce did not have enough time to produce engaging and active learning environments. Maybe we could use technology to make the classroom more efficient.

A solution for the education industry had to be a technology or strategy both easily understood and implemented so that it could catch on quickly. It also needed to be something that was inexpensive because school systems don't have a massive amount of money to spend on innovations.

Paperslide videos continued to grow in popularity. As a result of my presentations, now thousands of teachers and students were publishing paperslide artifacts of their learning. Because of this, I saw one-take videos as the most viable tool for classrooms. I looked closer at how teachers were using this strategy. Most of what I saw was that paperslide videos were assigned so that students would have the opportunity to reteach and explain information in their own words. This made me wonder: What if we had teachers use a similar strategy to record their lecture content? It would be a one-take lecture video.

SIT AND LOOK AT THE CAMERA

In early December 2010, I took my Flip camera out of my pocket, set it up on a heavy-duty tripod in one of the meeting rooms at the FI and pointed it at a wall-mounted whiteboard. I wrote a few diagrams and definitions on the whiteboard. The lesson was about demand, a topic that I had taught many times in a number of different classrooms. There were a handful of definitions and some graphs and tables ready to go on the board, within the frame of the shot. I looked over the information, mentally practicing my lesson delivery. After a few minutes, I hit record, sat down in front of the camera and started flailing my arms wildly while talking about demand. The room was empty and I was speaking loudly as if I was in a full classroom, referencing the information. I would look at the steady red light on the camera that indicated recording was taking place, then back at the whiteboard, then back at the red light, then back at the whiteboard, nervously. I was sweating and stammering. I had stage fright.

The whole lesson was extremely uncomfortable and felt like an eternity. Every "uh" or "um" and every hesitation while I tried to remember what to say seemed to be greatly amplified in that small, empty meeting room. Since it was a one-take video, I just let it roll, pushing through all the mistakes, teaching the lesson. When I was done, I stepped out of the shot thinking that I had just created the longest video ever. It used to take me around 55 minutes to lecture on this topic live in the classroom, multiple times a day.

I was convinced that this was absolutely not any type of solution. There was no way the video was going to be more efficient (shorter) than my live lecture on this topic. Also, right before hitting stop on the camera, I was worried that I had done a terrible job with the lesson. It was filled with mistakes, awkward hesitations, strange faces, and wild spastic gestures that would surely be distracting to my audience. I suddenly flashed back to when I was forced to record and watch myself teach during my student teaching placement. I knew watching this was going to be painful. I wanted to smash the camera on the ground, walk out the room, and never record myself teaching ever again. I didn't do that. Instead, I postponed my judgment.

I pressed the red button on the camera to stop recording. The digital timer on the screen showed that the video was 15:06. That couldn't be right. I thought something had gone wrong and that maybe the camera had recorded only half of the lecture. There was no way my entire presentation was only 15 minutes. It felt way longer.

I clicked play on the camera, and saw all the content on the screen. Then, I saw myself walk into the shot and start teaching the lesson. Immediately, I wished that I had combed my hair and worn a different shirt. It was extremely uncomfortable to watch myself on that screen. I panicked, and after 30 seconds, I shut the camera off. It was like there was someone screaming inside my head to delete the video and never look at it again. I hated what I saw.

In that 30 seconds, I saw the real me. I saw that my gestures were awkward and that I was fidgeting too much. I was much less skilled than I had convinced myself that I was in real life. In real life, I was the gold standard of teaching. In real life, I shined when I was explaining economics. In real life, teaching was my superpower. But on video, I was mediocre, at best. My heart was racing, and my ego was damaged.

I left the room and went outside to take a walk and collect my thoughts. During my 15-minute stroll I convinced myself that I needed to watch the entire video. I also remembered that we are our own worst critics, so I needed to watch it again and not be consumed with the things that bothered me. Instead, I needed to focus on whether the content was clear enough for others to understand it. I also talked myself into changing my mindset, so that I would be aware of the negatives, but I would allow myself to also look for what I did well. I knew that I could always re-record, working to remove what I did not like and doing more of what worked well.

I could justify doing all of this because I was alone in that room. I did not have anyone in there judging or evaluating me or my video. It was a completely safe environment for me to reflect on my work and make improvements. It was natural that I was experiencing some cognitive dissonance, confronted with this reality on video that conflicted with what I thought of myself, how I imagined myself to look while teaching.

I walked back into the meeting room and everything was just as I left it. I walked over to the camera, turned it on, and pressed play. I zeroed in on the same things again. I hated my hair, my clothes, the wild gesturing. But then I remembered that I was alone and this was a safe place. After a few moments, I got over that and could pay attention to how I was actually doing with my lesson delivery. I was trying to see the lesson through the eyes of a student. To my surprise, from that perspective, I was doing a decent job. For the most part I was clear and concise. All the little mistakes that I made seemed like a big deal in the moment, but I didn't even notice many of them on playback, once I changed my perspective. In fact, the ones I did notice seemed like very typical glitches that everyone experiences when teaching, or so I told myself.

There was a list of things that I definitely needed to change, from the way I explained some of the content to my physical behaviors. There were also good things like my enthusiasm and easy-to-follow examples.

I was focused on what I could do to better communicate the information. Watching it back both broke me down and built me up. I was reminded that I was not really a superhero. I was just a normal guy doing a decent job communicating some information. But this reflective process also gave me the power to make adjustments and improvements. Before reflecting, I was convinced that I was good. This recording was a rare opportunity to see the truth.

I watched it back two more times, continuing to make note of what I liked and what needed to be improved. I also went on YouTube and watched two other video lectures on the same topic created by other teachers. Then, I watched mine again. After about an hour of viewing and reflecting, I decided to just record it again and make the changes that I had outlined for myself. I was much more comfortable with the content and with the delivery after watching myself and seeing other examples.

I hit record. It was still a bit uncomfortable going through the information, but I felt much more confident in what I was saying. I finished, walked around the camera, pressed stop and saw that the timestamp read 13:50.[19] I had made my lesson about a minute shorter than the first take. I watched the new lesson back and was very pleased with my progress. It was much easier to watch because I had been able to fix some of the glaring issues that I saw in the first one (like less flailing with the arms). More work needed to be done on my presentation, but this was certainly a great step.

I was elated for another reason. It certainly was not the best-looking video in the world, but as I knew from winning the VMware contest and working with teachers to create paperslide videos, the quality and aesthetic was not important. If the content and message are strong, it's a great video. I would feel absolutely no compunction about publishing that video and sending it to my students. They would absolutely be able to learn the content from this 13:50 one-take lecture video. That is what mattered.

This video covered all the information I needed to say about demand. It covered all the necessary content that used to take me 55 minutes live in the classroom, but the video was only 13:50. I was beyond excited about this discovery because I had actually done it; I had solved the problem of time, right out of the gate on the first try. I had created time, and a lot of it.

I felt like a wizard. What used to take 55 minutes now only takes slightly under 14. And that would have been 14 minutes in period one, two, and four. If I was still teaching high school, I would not need to repeat this information three times a day. Instead of saying the same thing over and over for 165 minutes (55 minutes X three periods), I could just play the video, and all my classes would receive the exact same information. This creates a massive amount of time and would keep me from that mind-numbing repetition I experienced when I was teaching.

---

19 Demand (Originally recorded in 2011 but uploaded to YouTube in 2013). Retrieved from http://schooled.lodgemccammon.com

This was too good to be true. I needed to try it again. I combed my hair and changed my shirt (deciding to avoid wearing green in future videos, for some reason that color makes me look ill) and spent the rest of the day recording one-take lecture videos. It took me seven hours to record four videos in this style. As I completed each one, I had the familiar feeling that it was a very long video. Each time I walked around the camera to hit stop, I looked at the video length and realized that a ratio of 4:1 (live lecture:video lecture) seemed to be consistent. The four videos I recorded took me 50+ minutes to deliver live in the classroom. All the one-take video lectures of those lessons were between 10 and 14 minutes.

Eureka! This was like discovering the assembly line for the classroom. It was a way to make teaching extremely efficient. I was both bewildered and excited. I didn't really understand how it was possible to take a 50-minute live lecture and reduce it to around 12 minutes, but I knew it was important. With each new video I recorded and reflected on, I was reminded of my disbelief. To try and explain it, I thought back to when I taught these lessons and tried to figure out the big differences between my classroom with 32 students and this empty meeting room at the FI.

I decided that two main factors slowed down live lecture. First, interruptions. I thought about all the interruptions that happen in the classroom. They ranged from having to correct student behavior to constantly answering unrelated student questions. This slows down the delivery of content drastically. Second, since I had to lecture the same content multiple times a day, it exhausted and bored me. The video allowed me to express the content once as clearly as I could, and then it was done. No need to repeat it. I could just click play.

This was the most important breakthrough thus far in my career. I not only solved the problem of time using an $80 Flip camera and whiteboard, but I had figured out a strategy that could alleviate teachers' exhaustion, or at least it would have reduced my exhaustion when I was a teacher. If I had all my lectures recorded, I could have played them at the beginning of class and used the rest of class time to engage the students. If I had known this back in 2003, I probably would not have ended up in the hospital. I probably would not have ended up quitting. However, Flip cameras did not exist back then, and creating one-take videos was not as effortless as it was in 2010.

Over the course of the next several years, I recorded hundreds of one-take lecture videos for a variety of content areas and grade levels. After completing each one, I would watch it back and make note of what I did well and what I needed to improve upon. I would then try and use that information to make my next one better. This simple reflective practice routine drastically improved my communication skills, allowing me to become a much better teacher. I used the process to decrease my cognitive dissonance, in the attempt to line up what I think about myself with what was on the screen. I am still working toward that goal, but this form of reflective practice is the best way to see yourself for who you are and what you can do, so you can reach your true potential. Do you want to be the best teacher you can be? The most powerful way I've found to achieve that is to dedicate a part of your life to the one-take video recording and reflecting process.[20]

After creating those first few videos, I thought, "Surely someone had figured this out already." This is too big of a discovery to be hidden all these years, especially since we have had the technology to make it work for some time (Flip cameras came out around 2007). I did some research and found that the practice of teachers creating and using video to deliver classroom content had been studied for many years. There was a significant amount of information that outlines some of the benefits of using video for instruction. This field of study is called "self-paced learning." Essentially, lesson content is made available to students anywhere, any time, and in a way that can be consumed as many times as necessary in order for a student to process the information. It makes all the sense in the world. The research suggested

---

20 You Are Your Best Teacher. Retrieved from http://schooled.lodgemccammon.com

that if we can record our lecture content and offer it to students in a self-paced way, it could increase student achievement.

MIND-BLOWING

In eighth grade, I had a history teacher named Mr. Kinny. He would lecture from bell to bell, 45 minutes every day. He was super boring. His tests were on his lectures. It was extremely difficult for me to pay attention during his lectures, so I ended up missing a lot of the notes. Therefore, I did not do very well on the tests. I realized that if Mr. Kinny could have recorded his lecture content, it would have been nearly 75 percent shorter than him just babbling in front of the class every day. If he could have played his 11-minute video at the beginning of the period, we could then do anything other than listen to him talk for the remaining 34 minutes. To top it off, I would have been able to go back and watch those 11-minute videos over and over to gather all the notes and study for the tests. I could have been a straight A student (OK, maybe B+). I might have even liked eighth grade social studies! Instead, I got a C and hated it.

Let's remember though, back when I was in school, videos were very difficult to record with clunky, expensive cameras. They were even more difficult to distribute via handing over VHS tapes. Those days were over. Many of us have high-definition video cameras in our pockets. We can record, upload and share videos effortlessly. In fact, many of us do this every day. We record and share videos of our cats, kids, food and varied activities. And that same camera in our pockets doubles as our viewing device. What I was realizing in 2010 is that teachers can use this same process to start an educational revolution similar to how the assembly line accelerated the industrial revolution.

The one-take video lecture strategy was critical for lowering the barrier so that literally any teacher with a Flip camera, or something similar, could start creating a self-paced learning environment for their students tomorrow. We must remember what I learned from my dissertation and my years of travel working with thousands of educators: Most teachers are not interested in, nor do they have time to learn, complex video editing software or techniques.

I also started thinking that even though the one-take lecture videos are easily created, it would take a lot of time for every teacher to create one for every single lecture they are responsible for giving. In fact, based on what I created so far, each video lecture took me well over an hour to record, reflect on, and publish. There are around 60 lectures that I delivered for my APECON class. That means that I will likely need to spend 70+ hours to create one-take videos for all my content.

Any major change takes a lot of work. I knew that recording and reflecting on this content would change my life. I would be looking at myself honestly and critically. This would give me an opportunity to drastically improve my communication skills. This process would push me toward reaching my potential as a teacher. It was worth 70 hours of work. And, it continues to be worth the thousands of hours I have spent recording and reflecting since.

Allow me to make a comparison. Let's say you want to lose 50 pounds and you believe that would significantly change your life. It's going to take a lot of focus, changes to your regular diet, exercise, and willpower to achieve that goal. Is it worth all that effort to lose 50 pounds? If the answer is yes, then the work is worth it. We have a similar issue here. Creating your lesson content, making your information delivery more efficient, and offering your students a self-paced learning environment is going to take a lot of work. Based on the research, it can have a positive impact on student retention of the information and student achievement. If that's important to you, then the work is worth it.

You might be thinking, "This dude must be super old and has never heard of the internets or the worldwide webs." You may say, "If he knew anything about the internet, he would know that there are sites like YouTube that have thousands of lecture videos that cover almost any topic taught in school. In fact, he probably doesn't even know about Khan Academy. Teachers don't have to do any work to make this happen – all the video content it takes to do this is already on the internet."

Well, if I may respond, in fact I have heard of the internet. Yes, there is a lot of content online, likely multiple videos on every topic taught in school. Where this breaks down is that education relies on a relationship between teacher and student. If students don't think the teacher cares about them, the learning breaks down. If a teacher outsources the delivery of content, that can break down the relationship between teacher and student.[21]

Have you ever had a substitute teacher try and teach a lesson? It rarely goes well. Oftentimes, after students encounter a substitute, upon their regular teacher returning, they will say something like, "We are glad you're back. We had no clue what that sub was talking about." Outsourcing the delivery of your content to another teacher on the internet will likely have a similar outcome.

I am surely not saying that all those other lecture videos on the internet are useless. In fact, they can be extremely valuable resources. The smartest teachers that I know will go online and find the best video on a topic, similar to what I did when I completed my first video about demand. They watch an alternative explanation and make note of aspects they want to integrate into their own lesson. Then, they record their version by integrating all the best ideas while still customizing it for their unique classroom and students.

Then, I found out that lots of teachers were already doing this.

---

21 Katie v. Khan Academy. Retrieved from http://schooled.lodgemccammon.com

CHAPTER 14

Flipping the Classroom

• • •

It's January 2011 and I now know that having teachers record one-take video lectures is an efficient and simple solution to the problem of time. While I was celebrating my burgeoning intellect, I did a bit more internet research on the topic. I already knew there was a solid research foundation for the practice, but I wanted to know what kind of teachers were using video to create self-paced learning environments, now that it was so easy to create and distribute video content.

The phrase I kept encountering was "flipping the classroom." This term was consistently used to describe a seemingly prescriptive practice of assigning students to watch video lectures for homework. Then, students would come into the classroom, having watched the videos, effectively removing the lecture portion of class. The teacher would use the freed-up class time to allow the students to apply their learning and ask questions. The "flipped" part of flipping the classroom meant that we were flipping what was for homework and what was for class work. Thus, the lecture became homework, and the homework became the in-class work.

Upon first-time reading about flipping the classroom, I thought that it was just the higher education model of learning, renamed. In graduate school, the classes would be structured so that the students would read a chapter from a text for homework. Then, in class, the professor would answer questions and lead a discussion about that information.

Incidentally, I only had a very small number of classes where the professor pulled this off successfully. What usually happened was that the professor would assign the readings for homework, then during class time, the professor would lecture for an hour, talking about what the students read the night before. This did not encourage students to continue to read in preparation for class. There was no incentive to do so if the professor was going to lecture on the content anyway.

A few years before I started looking into these flipped classrooms, two teachers from Colorado had coined the phrase "flipping the classroom." Jonathan Bergmann and Aaron Sams taught high school chemistry and had video recorded their lecture content and offered it to students to create a self-paced learning environment. They used a rather complex screen recording software to generate their video content, and they were having students watch the videos for homework. In class, students were working collaboratively on labs and activities. They received some press about this teaching practice, and discussed the benefits for students.

At this time, I also ran across a TED Talk given by Salmon Khan, creator of the Khan Academy. The title of his talk was "Let's Use Video to Reinvent Education." He had created thousands of video lectures and posted them to YouTube for free. He discussed the power of self-paced learning and suggested that teachers use his videos to allow students to move through the content at their own speed. He wanted teachers to outsource their content delivery in order to flip their classrooms. His videos had millions of views, but I could not find many classroom teachers who were using his videos that way, to successfully replace their lecture entirely.

Finally, also in 2011, I learned about a school outside Detroit called Clintondale High School. The principal, Greg Green, had promoted the flipped classroom methodology and was touting the first fully flipped school. Teachers at Clintondale recorded video lectures and offered students access to them both inside and outside of school. This freed-up class time to engage students with active learning environments. Student success increased, and Greg got some national attention for leading this charge.

I was enthused that this teaching practice was starting to be widely discussed among educators and in the popular press. It had some features that mapped with my solution. Specifically, it was great that more educators were using videos to change how time was spent in the classroom. I even liked the moniker "flipping the classroom." It's fun to say and at the time we were touting the use of Flip cameras for creating low-barrier one-take videos. I jumped on the flipped classroom bandwagon.

While there were lots of people talking about this teaching method at this time, there were not any resources (that I could find) that helped educators make the change to a flipped classroom. That's where I wanted to contribute. I wanted to provide the research justification for the teaching practice, as well as design and offer simple training materials that allowed educators low-barrier ways to experiment with this self-paced and efficient teaching method.

KATIE GIMBAR

If I wanted to get the word out to educators about my solution, it was time to get a little honest with myself. I was 34 years old in 2011. I had been out of the classroom for almost a decade. I had a Ph.D. and worked at a fancy university think tank. The harsh truth was that I was not relatable. I was an academic, and thus my impact on practice would be limited because I would be seen as someone bringing ideas down from that pesky ivory tower.

What I really needed was an actual classroom teacher to use the method every day, so I could document the experience, understand the challenges, and show off the benefits of the method in a real classroom. Teachers needed to see it work, not just hear about it theoretically from some guy with a Ph.D. who referred to himself as Dr. Lodge.

So, what features would this teacher need to have? Well, I figured I should probably search for a female teacher because women represent about 75 percent of the workforce. I would want her to be young, as I thought that this type of innovation in teaching would appeal largely to younger educators (which, in retrospect was not always the case). Finally, she would need to be intelligent, passionate about teaching and be open to change. As I wrote down this list of attributes, I knew that it described Ms. C from my dissertation. However, she had been recruited out of education two years earlier by a biofuels company to do corporate training, so she was not an option.

In early January 2011, I reached out to my friend and former assistant, Luke (he was the student I hired back in 2007 with the VMware money), who was now a social studies teacher at Durant Road Middle School in Wake County. I sent him an email with the list of attributes and told him I was looking for a teacher who met all of them. He responded almost immediately and told me to look no further than right down the hall from his classroom.

Luke went on to describe Katie Gimbar as a total rock star. He said that she was a young, smart, passionate teacher who the students absolutely adored. She had been teaching for about four years and it just so happened that she taught Algebra 1. He gave me her email address and I immediately sent her a message, asking if I could come observe her classroom. She replied within a few minutes and said that I was welcome whenever I wanted to visit.

Two days later I walked into Katie Gimbar's classroom at Durant Road Middle School and was blown away by two things. First, she was great with the kids, and they truly did adore her. Her no nonsense but caring personality was spot on for winning the students over. Second, she had absurdly large classes. In one class, she had over 40 students, 11 of which had been moved in halfway through the year. These students had been in a regular eighth grade math class, but had recently been identified (by a standardized assessment) as likely to be successful in Algebra 1. So, after the holiday break, they were moved up.

With more than 40 students in the room, she was doing her best to essentially teach two different classes. She would spend a little time delivering new content to her regular Algebra 1 students, give those students some problems to work on and then transition to a different lesson working with the 11 new additions, attempting to get them up to speed. Given that this was a nightmare scenario, she was doing the best job that could be expected.

After watching all her classes that day, we had a chance to chat. By this point, I had created my own series of videos that explained the basics and benefits (it was all stick figures and theory) of using one-take video to flip the classroom. Instead of spending time telling her about the idea face-to-face, I showed her one of my videos and encouraged her to ask questions.

The video I showed her was about 90 seconds long.[22] Incidentally, this would have taken me five minutes to explain the same information live and I told her that right before it started. The video briefly discussed how video lectures were a more efficient way to get through the required content and how they created a self-paced learning environment. The video ended with me stating that the time freed-up in the classroom could be used to engage students with an active learning environment. Katie watched this video diligently. After it was over, she turned to me and said that she only had one question: "When can I start?"

---

22 Flipping the Classroom. Retrieved from http://schooled.lodgemccammon.com

She believed that this would be the solution to so many issues she was currently having in her classroom. The main one was that if she had all her lecture content recorded, it would give her time to differentiate instruction. Differentiated instruction is simply modifying instruction (e.g., speed, difficulty, type) based on the needs of individual students. Essentially, it's all about personalizing the learning experience. She said, "Just the time it takes to cover the content gets in the way of being able to differentiate."

Throughout the spring of 2011, Katie visited the FI on weekends and her days off to record lecture content. While she was creating and recording, I either observed the process, assisted with her creations or spent time recording my own one-take videos. It was a factory of content creation. We found that the same ratio I uncovered, about 4:1 live to video lecture time, applied to her lecture videos as well. Katie would frequently complete a video and say, "I can't believe that I spent 40 minutes, multiple times a day, for four years, just repeating this content when the video is 10 minutes long." She recorded 85 videos over the course of four months. It took her about 120 hours to complete this one-take video lecture series.[23]

Let's do some math. The average length of her one-take video lectures was 10 minutes. That means she created about 850 minutes of video lecture content. The average length of these lectures delivered live for these 85 topics was 40 minutes. That means it previously took Katie 3,400 minutes to cover the same information live in the classroom. Considering the fact that she repeated the same lecture multiple times per day, and had to do it year after year, we are looking at an incredible shift in efficiency.

Repeat 3,400 minutes of lecture every year or click play on 850 minutes? Which would you choose? Not only that, but Katie would be taking advantage of the fact that these videos, published to YouTube,

---

23   A Katie Gimbar Playlist. Retrieved from http://schooled.lodgemccammon.com

would allow the students to learn in a self-paced way, whenever and wherever. It was such a massive win.

Katie started using the videos in class right away (projecting them in the classroom and allowing students to watch them on the classroom computers). The benefits were precisely what she had hoped. In her class of more than 40 students, she was able to assign the two different groups (the 11 who were added and the other 30) to watch two different lecture video presentations. After each group watched their lecture, she had time to put them in groups and differentiate instruction. Students who needed to watch her lectures two or three times to process the information could do so. Students who missed class would quickly catch back up by watching a 10-minute video on a computer in the back of the room at the beginning of class while the other students started their differentiated assignments. It was an extremely flexible learning environment.

Throughout the spring semester, Katie used her videos in all her classes with great success. For example, the 11 students who had been added to her Algebra 1 class halfway through the year all passed the end of course exam. None of them scored lower than an 80 percent. Thus, students who had essentially missed half of a year in a course were not only able to catch up, but they were able to excel because she offered them a self-paced and active learning environment.

All her students benefited from this teaching method. Katie regularly said that in the four years that she had been teaching, she had never had time to truly differentiate instruction. Now, using the one-take method of flipping the classroom, she was able to differentiate every day because it created so much time.

Katie and I frequently got together to discuss how the process was going and what adjustments needed to be made. I would visit her classroom regularly to observe. Sometimes I would drop by her room and participate in the lesson, so I could experience the teaching method from the student perspective.

It was unlike anything I'd ever experienced before. I would come into the classroom as a student. Katie would play a 10-minute video while we took notes. Then, she would break us up into groups and give us some problems to work on. We would spend about 30 minutes discussing and solving problems, taking advantage of collaboration and peer teaching. During the 30 minutes, Katie would visit each group to manage behavior, answer questions, and assess our understanding of the content. In the last few minutes of class, Katie would wrap up and remind us that the video we watched is online if we needed to review it. It was pure efficiency and active learning. The time went by so quickly during those class periods because learning was not boring.

Katie ended up experimenting with all different ways of using the one-take video lectures as a self-paced learning tool for the students. She would have students watch them both inside and outside the classroom.[24]

Within the spring semester, after the students had adjusted to this new way of learning, Katie started to tell me that, for the first time, she had a significant amount of extra class time. She was flying through the content. Student attitudes, comprehension, engagement and scores were improving, even with her huge class sizes. She was actually ahead of the pacing guide. She finally had time to try some new and innovative techniques. She had time to change the way she thought about instruction.

This was an exciting thing for me to hear. Remember when I created that music-based Algebra 1 curriculum? Remember that most of the math teachers said that none of them had time to do any of it? Well, now Katie was coming to me and saying that she had *too much* time. She said that she was looking for activities that would engage and challenge her students

---

24 Katie Gimbar's Classroom. Retrieved from http://schooled.lodgemccammon.com

in new ways. She was interested in continuing to make changes to her instruction.

Katie started using my music-based curriculum. Her students were creating one-take music videos to my songs about the quadratic formula and exponential functions. They were creating paperslide videos to re-teach (in their own words) concepts like systems of equations and slope. It was awesome!

She was even having some of her advanced students create their own one-take lecture videos on topics like inequalities and two-step equations. Almost every time I observed or participated in her classroom, after we got done watching one of Katie's lecture videos, a student would ask, "When do we get to create our own videos like that?" Her response was always the same. She said, "You can create them if you master the content first." The promise of creation drove many students to excel.

Let's not forget that these videos were not fancy. They were not flashy. They were created with an $80 Flip camera pointed at a few whiteboards. However, students saw their teacher up on that screen and wanted to be great like that. They were inspired by the excellent work their teacher was doing.

Though Katie already had a great relationship with her students, it seemed that their relationship somehow improved. Many started re-ferring to her as "YouTube famous." I thought this was a great pe-ripheral benefit of creating one-take video lectures, especially given what we know about the importance of the teacher-student relation-ship on learning. Recording and publishing lecture content seemed like a turnkey method for building trust. I even heard an eighth grader in the hallway one day boast to another student, "Is your teacher on YouTube? Mine is and she is awesome."

After seeing her success in that first semester of flipped teaching, the other three Algebra 1 teachers on Katie's team at Durant Road Middle School started creating their own one-take video lectures. They followed the same teaching model, offering students an efficient and self-paced lecture content. They used the freed-up class time to create an active and differentiated learning environment. Eventually, they even used some of my music-based curriculum. Her team started to see the same benefits.

It was so great that I had four teachers doing this. Now, I just needed the other three million to get on board. Easier said than done.

CHAPTER 15

Scale

• • •

I WAS CONVINCED THAT I had identified the main problem with education: Teachers don't have time to create active learning environments for their students. I had established a research-based and practical method for creating time. I had tested the solution in the field. It worked brilliantly, and I documented everything.

In addition, if I am being honest, I had figured out what I set out to figure out. I knew now why I had failed as a teacher. The teaching practices that I used to deliver content to my students were absurdly inefficient. Having to keep up with the pacing guide while repeating myself all day every day was exhausting. Those rare times when I would challenge my students to be active in their learning were great, but it would burn through too much class time, resulting in me being behind on the pacing guide. This was my downward spiral. I was constantly exhausted and stressed, which landed me in the hospital.

Here I was, a decade later, touting a teaching method that alleviated all those issues, and it could be achieved using the camera on my cell phone and a free YouTube account. Incredible.

So, where do I go from here? Should I go back and teach? Should I move on to something else? After pondering for a while, I decided to see if I could scale what I had developed. I wanted to spread the use of the method and help other teachers avoid what I had gone through. This decision reminded me of being the head of the sunshine committee (back at Wakefield). As such, my primary goal was to try and increase the job satisfaction by spreading happiness. Instead of spreading happiness, I would be spreading efficiency. After all, an efficient life can certainly be a happy life.

Marketing

As Katie became more and more comfortable with the teaching method, we started recording videos to show and explain how her classroom worked. I documented her students watching the lecture videos in class, working in groups and explaining how they used the videos at home. I wanted to create a series of videos that would make her classroom and this method completely transparent. I wanted to help as many people as possible.

I had Katie record a "Why I Flipped My Classroom" video explaining the basic concept and benefits.[25] In the video, she explains that before flipping her classroom, she was spending 90 percent of her class time on content delivery and 10 percent on active learning. She continues by explaining that after recording and publishing her content, she was able to spend 90 percent of her class time on active learning and only 10 percent on content delivery. The other teachers on her team were experiencing the same shift.

Because of these percentages, I started to divert from the popular explanation of a flipped classroom. To me, it seemed that the engine powering a flipped classroom was *not* that students were watching videos for homework (forcing students to watch videos for homework can be problematic), it's the fact that the video lectures are a much more efficient and effective method for delivering lecture content; the flip is in efficiency.

---

25 Why I Flipped My Classroom. Retrieved from http://schooled.lodgemccammon.com

I found out quickly that aligning this work with the growing "flipped classroom" movement was both good and bad. Good because as soon as I said, "flipped classroom," many educators were somewhat familiar with the concept and would say something like, "That's where teachers assign students to watch videos for homework." It's bad because most of the time those same teachers would then say, "That would never work for me because my students don't have access to the internet outside of school, and even if they did, they would not watch the videos for homework." I always found it interesting that so many people would vehemently explain how something they have never tried could not possibly work.

I would go blue in the face telling people that the flipped classroom is more about the efficient delivery of the content than it is about having students watch videos for homework. I would continue by saying that every 40-minute live lecture can be reduced to a 10-minute video. I went on to say, "Videos don't have to be homework. Simply show that video in class and then use the extra 30 minutes to challenge students to be active in their learning." Many teachers would look at me funny and say, "Lots of my students don't have internet at home so I can't flip my classroom."

The comments and questions were endless. "What if students don't watch the videos?" "How do you assess student understanding of the videos?" "Can I use someone else's videos?" "How long do the videos need to be?" "Do we need to train the students to watch the videos?" On and on. And on. Katie and I would answer many of these questions every time we had a conversation or gave a presentation about our flipped classroom method. "I wish there was some way to keep from repeating the same information over and over," I thought to myself. Oh, wait.

I assembled the most common questions and asked Katie to record a series of "frequently asked questions" videos using the one-take video lecture strategy. I recorded a few as well. I published these videos on my

YouTube channel and shared them publicly.[26] The idea was that we could point educators toward a playlist of these videos if they wanted to learn more about the method, based on some of the common questions we received. Just like delivering content in a classroom, these videos were an efficient solution for delivering information, saving us from hours of repeating ourselves.

As the discussion around the flipped classroom started to take off internationally, so did the views on our videos. It seemed like everywhere we went (for educational purposes), people would say, "I've seen some of your videos. I feel like I know you!" Katie would occasionally tell me about a teacher who stopped her in the grocery store and said that he or she recognized her from YouTube. How cool is that?

Because of the popularity of our YouTube videos, I started getting emails requesting that Katie and I speak at schools and conferences. We started traveling around the country speaking about what we had created. We were even invited to speak at a TEDx event put on by NCSU.

These TEDx events are interesting. They typically consist of a series of rapid-fire keynote-style talks given by different people over the course of a day. These talks, which are usually on a variety of topics, are recorded and published online so that the information can be shared with the world. The TED catchphrase is "ideas worth sharing." The intention is to create a stage where people can share how they have solved problems. It's a pretty cool concept.

Katie and I decided to do a collaborative presentation called "Flipping the Classroom with FIZZ." That means that we would be on stage at the same time. I would talk about the research foundations of the teaching method and she would talk about implementing it in the classroom. We put together a PowerPoint presentation and practiced a few times to make

---

26 FAQ. Retrieved from http://schooled.lodgemccammon.com

sure it was less than 18 minutes (the maximum time allowed for a TED presentation), and then we were ready to present. I even made custom t-shirts. Hers had a picture of me on it and mine had a picture of her. I figured that it would be funny. I'm not sure that it was.

Photo by Kylie Cafiero

This was the first time that one of my more formal presentations was going to be recorded. Because I had recorded so many one-take videos, I figured it would not be a problem. In actuality, it was a problem. Right before we got on stage, I got strangely nervous. I knew that TEDx talks were a pretty big deal. People paid attention to them, and they were published on YouTube. I felt a considerable amount of pressure and this pressure made me panic a little.

The talk was over before we knew it, and I thought that we did all right. A few people from the audience approached me and said that they enjoyed the presentation. Friends that came to watch said it was good. However, a few days later I got to know the truth because the video was posted online.[27]

I sat and watched it on my cell phone and was horrified. It was exactly the same feeling I had when I watched myself teach for the first time. It was the same as when I created my first one-take video lecture. My hair was a mess. My shirt looked silly. When it was my turn to talk, I paced nervously across the stage. I did this so much and so quickly that sometimes the cameraman was not able to keep up. It was brutal to watch because I looked really uncomfortable.

Fortunately, Katie looked great and was as cool as a cucumber. She did a fantastic job and it balanced out my ridiculousness. To this day, I still can't watch that video. I watched it that one time to reflect and I got a lot out of it. I decided to record all my presentations from then on, so I could improve. But I don't need to relive that one.

While I didn't have any marketing experience, my main strategy was to create and publish practical video resources on YouTube for free. When educators viewed, used and shared the videos, some would reach out and ask us to present. These presentations would allow us to engage with large audiences in order to model the one-take flipped classroom strategies, really getting the audiences hooked on the concept. As audiences got hooked, they would view and share our videos even more. The cycle would continue.

This all worked because the method was an easy sell. It was scalable. Any teacher could make a huge upgrade to their classroom and only needed

---

27 Flipping the Classroom with FIZZ. Retrieved from
http://schooled.lodgemccammon.com

a video camera, a few whiteboards and access to YouTube (or similar video-hosting site). By the way, we absolutely encouraged the use of YouTube because there seemed to be an incredible social value for a teacher "being on YouTube." In the many conversations I had with students, the phrase, "My teacher is YouTube famous" was not uncommon. We had a simple formula for a powerful outcome.

An Opinion Editorial

In early 2012, Katie and I wrote an Opinion Editorial (op-ed), with help from two colleagues who worked for NCSU News Services. The News & Observer, the largest newspaper in Raleigh and the same one that interviewed me back in 2004 about how I used music in the classroom, picked up the op-ed. In it, Katie and I discussed how the one-take flipped method of teaching Algebra 1 was superior to the traditional method of live lecture. At the time there was a lot of focus on getting students to be successful in math, thus the editorial received some attention.

The day that the op-ed was published, I received a few angry emails. Some concerned citizens wrote things like, "Students won't learn if you teach this way" and "It's ideas like this that are ruining the education system." Yikes! Really? There was no downside to this teaching method that I had seen. It was useful for every type of learner in Katie's classroom. Yet, some people got upset.

I was convinced that my method was bulletproof, but just to be safe, I used this as an opportunity to dig through the literature and shared additional research that continued to provide a solid foundation for why this method was great for all teachers and students.[28] Additionally, I just assumed that this was how life was going to be and I was fine with it. I found out that as soon as you start marketing different ideas and getting

---

28 Flipped Classroom Research. Retrieved from http://schooled.lodgemccammon.com

attention, people come out of the woodwork to try and tear you down.[29] It's the nature of the beast. However, I don't want you to think I only received negative emails. I started receiving scores of very nice messages thanking us for the free resources that we had created. Then, we got the best email of them all.

GOODNIGHT MONEY

The day after our editorial was published, Ann Goodnight, wife of Jim Goodnight who is co-founder and CEO of SAS (a statistical software company in North Carolina's Research Triangle), contacted Katie. Ann reached out to Katie to say that she found the article compelling and asked if she could come by and observe the flipped classroom in action. Katie, of course, said yes and told her she was welcome to come by anytime.

The Goodnights are long-time supporters of NCSU. More specifically, the Goodnights donated a large portion of money to develop the FI, where I was currently working, and Ann was on the board of directors. I would be willing to bet they were in blue or black suits, standing outside the FI during that ribbon cutting ceremony back in 2005 that I almost crashed in my shorts and t-shirt.

The Goodnights have also funded a number of other programs and projects that aim to improve education across North Carolina, including founding Cary Academy, an independent prep school. To that end, SAS has an entire education department that develops resources and training materials for teachers all over the world. It was extremely exciting that our article had caught the attention of likely the biggest education advocate in the state.

This was additionally interesting because even though Ann was on the FI board of directors, and I worked at the FI, she was likely not aware of

---

29 The Crab Mentality. Retrieved from http://schooled.lodgemccammon.com

my project before reading about it in the paper. At this point, Katie and I had been working together for about a year and had done a handful of keynotes, workshops and presentations around the country. Our YouTube videos had hundreds of thousands of views and a handful of teachers around North Carolina had implemented our teaching model. However, the board of directors at the FI was probably not aware of this work. Was it because the FI was a huge organization? Nope.

This was on purpose. The FI was part of the university. The university was in the business of getting big grants. The idea was that a professor would get a grant, let's say $5 million dollars, to study an educational topic or develop a process. The university would take maybe 50 percent of that money off the top. The professor would do the grant work and then use the success of completing the grant to get another grant. That's part of how a university keeps the lights on. To be clear, I am not judging this business model. It's a business model that has worked for a long time.

My business model was different. I worked to rapidly create and publish free online resources that helped teachers make significant changes to their day-to-day instruction. By publishing free resources, I could become well-known and organizations, districts and schools could hire me to give speeches or facilitate presentations and workshops.

It could be said that my work was the opposite of the university business model. As a result, I was told by my peers and even my boss that my work "did not belong at the FI," so I was not normally invited to participate in things like leadership meetings or presentations to the board of directors. However, Ann Goodnight could learn about my work by reading about it in the paper and once again, the News & Observer hooked me up with a very cool opportunity.

Ann observed Katie's classroom and was extremely impressed with the work. She saw a very standard public school classroom packed with

35 students, working in groups on differentiated assignments. She talked to a number of students who praised this new method of learning for a variety of reasons, such as having the ability to revisit their teacher's lecture as many times as they needed to be successful on the quizzes and tests. Each one reported that their grades improved as a result. Statements like these certainly echoed the research about the benefits of self-paced learning.

After her visit to Katie's classroom, Ann called the FI and donated a large sum of money to my project so that I could focus on scaling what Katie was doing in her classroom (it was not considered a grant, but just a personal donation). She wanted to see more teachers, classrooms and schools in North Carolina using these methods to engage all learners.

THE FLIPPED CLASSROOM TRAINING PROGRAM (FOR TEACHERS)

It's 2012. At this point, some of you might be wondering why I am bothering with all of this mess. Why bother getting money, trying to expand the teaching practice and convincing others of the solution? I set out to uncover why I failed as a teacher. It took me about a decade at this point, but I had it nailed down. I had identified that the biggest problem in education was the lack of time educators had to implement new teaching strategies. I had designed a simple, efficient and scalable solution that was extremely inexpensive. I had made a series of videos that explained the concept, showed it working in a classroom and answered all the frequently asked questions. I could have easily just clapped my hands, done a funky dance and walked away knowing that I had gone above and beyond what I had set out to do. I totally could have, but there were two things keeping that from happening.

First, I noticed that the more videos I created and the more attention they received, the more people contacted me to come speak at schools, conferences and events. Getting an email that said, "I saw your videos on YouTube, and we want you to speak" was addictive. Those emails were more and more frequent. Also, I really enjoyed these speaking gigs and was getting better at them. Facilitating presentations, workshops and keynotes allowed me to continue modeling all the different strategies that I had developed.

Speaking gigs handed me a classroom for the day and allowed me to continue experimenting. And by this point I was recording all of my speeches, presentations and workshops. Regardless of the venue or length, I would put a camera up in the corner and record a one-take video of the whole thing.[30] After it was over, I would watch it, making note of what I did well and what I could do to improve. I was obsessed with this method of reflective practice. If I wanted to improve, I needed to know how I was really doing. I could have listened to the people who said I did a great job or read Twitter posts about my speech, but watching a video of it opened my mind to what I needed to work on.

So, the logic here was that if we took this money from the Goodnights and built a teacher training program, scaling what was happening in Katie's classroom, more people would discover what I was doing, and I would be booked for more speaking engagements. The more speaking engagements I had, the more I would get to reflect on my practice. And the more I reflected, the more I would improve. And, of course, all of this would help teachers as well.

The second reason I kept doing this work was because the more teachers I talked to, the more I realized that Katie's model was not enough to convince everyone. This was a bitter pill to swallow because I believed that every single teacher should have been able to look at the videos that we had created and make the mental leap to easily integrate it into their classroom. It was not a complicated concept.

---

30 Presentation Timelapse. Retrieved from http://schooled.lodgemccammon.com

What we were really saying was that every teacher should take the information that they say to students (all the stuff they want students to know, the lecture part) and record it using the video camera in their pocket. Once they record it, teachers could simply publish it somewhere and give students the link. The videos on that playlist will be much shorter than saying the same information live. Then, teachers can use the freed-up time to do anything other than lecture to the kids. I mean, there you have it. Simple, right? Nope.

We constantly had elementary teachers come up after professional development sessions and say, "I don't see how this could possibly work in elementary classrooms." We had high school teachers come up and say, "This won't work in my high school classroom. This is only a middle school thing." We had middle school science, social studies, and language arts teachers come up and say, "I see how this could work in math, but I don't think it would work for my content area." That went on and on. I heard versions of those comments hundreds of times. Many of those teachers who were asking questions and making those statements seemed like they just didn't want to do it. Many teachers I encountered would spend endless mental energy finding reasons why it might not work for them instead of just trying it. It was frustrating.

I realized that if I wanted the teaching methods to spread, having Katie as a model wouldn't be enough. I needed teachers from different grades, different content areas, different types of schools and classrooms.

These two reasons fueled my passion for using the Goodnight money to build a training program for North Carolina teachers. Katie and I decided to offer a series of face-to-face training sessions at the FI for any North Carolina teachers who wanted to attend.

I assembled a 40-hour training program with Katie's help that teachers completed over three consecutive Saturdays. We decided upon 40 hours after interviewing a dozen or so teachers in the area who were using the teaching method every day. During the interviews, they seemed to agree that getting the first 20 lecture videos recorded and published was the biggest hurdle and the steepest learning curve. After that, it was much easier. So, we took that information and designed a training program that would require teachers to record their first 20 lecture videos, along with learning more about what to do with the freed-up class time. The training ended up requiring about 40 hours of work.

Trainees would be required to spend 20 hours at the FI recording one-take lecture videos and learning how to use them based on Katie's classroom model. They would also be required to spend an additional 20 hours outside the training reflecting on their video lectures, planning new lessons to record, and watching our lecture videos, including the how-to videos and frequently asked questions. This format would allow us to model flipped classroom strategies, making our training program an extremely efficient and active learning experience. We had the plan. Now, we just needed some teachers.

To get the word out, at the behest of Ann Goodnight, SAS emailed a large group of teachers in Wake, Durham, Johnston, and Orange counties, letting them know that they could sign up for the free training, sponsored by the FI and SAS. We offered three separate training sessions from July 2012 to October 2012 and accepted 40 teachers into the program.

These Saturday trainings were intense.[31] The sessions started at 9 a.m. and would go until 3 p.m. with a working lunch. Keep in mind that these were Saturdays during the school year. These 40 brave educators would spend all week teaching and then spend their Saturday in a full day of training. The dedication was impressive as was the variety of educators. We had elementary, middle, and high school teachers from all the core subject areas (math, science, social studies, and language arts). I was

---

31 Training Overview. Retrieved from http://schooled.lodgemccammon.com

thrilled that they saw enough value in this teaching method to spend part of their weekend creating materials and discussing how to make it work in their classrooms. They all had the problem of time and showed up on Saturday to learn how to solve it.

We maintained a fairly consistent structure throughout the training sessions. Teachers came prepared with their video outlines with the goal of creating seven lecture videos. Katie and I would use part of the morning to model flipped classroom strategies and then the teachers would have the rest of the day to record, chat and ask questions. Of course, we had a table in the corner of the room that was covered with all sorts of snacks and beverages. Snacks were critical for keeping the energy up! On that front, right around 11:30 a.m. each teacher would write down what they wanted from Jimmy John's and we would order lunch. About 30 minutes later the sandwiches would arrive and people would be happy. I ate more than 20 beach club sandwiches from Jimmy John's over the course of these training weekends. That's a lot of guacamole. Maybe too much?

This training format allowed a few really interesting things to happen. Teachers would show up on Saturday to discuss and create. Most of them focused on creating materials that they would then use in their classroom the following week. That meant that the next Saturday, when they came back, they could talk about which strategies worked or didn't work. These discussions were fascinating.

I overheard stories about how the videos solved so many practical classroom issues. Students who were absent would not have to miss the content. Students with learning disabilities were more successful because they were able to slow down the delivery of the content by pausing the videos. Students who were learning English as a second language could watch the videos multiple times to process the information, helping their language acquisition. Parents would send messages to the teachers, thanking them for making their teaching transparent.

Connecting with parents was the most widely discussed topic during these training days. The videos provided a way for teachers to build strong relationships with parents on a day-to-day basis. Parents would pull up the videos at home and watch them with their child to reinforce the content. Parents would meet with teachers about a student with disabilities and praise the math teacher for making videos so their child could finally slow down the content. And then they would ask why the other teachers were not making videos. It seemed that getting parents on board with what was happening in the classroom was a big win, and sending these videos home was a simple and powerful way of getting parents involved.

Each week during the training, the teachers were required to record and reflect on seven one-take lecture videos. This meant that they all went through the cognitive dissonance of seeing themselves on video, over and over. At first, everyone was uncomfortable doing this for the same reasons I was when I started, but Katie and I encouraged them to keep recording and improving. Every teacher drastically improved his or her communication skills and self-awareness using this reflection model. We would see amazing growth between their first video and their 20th. In some cases, it was extreme, and a whole new teacher emerged at the end of the training.

Because nearly every teacher was using the content they created each Saturday in their classrooms throughout the week, this meant that we could ask them about how the video lectures compared to their live lectures of the same information. The elementary teachers reported that their live lectures were five times longer than their video lectures; the ratio was 5:1. The middle and high school teachers reported that the ratio was 4:1, which is exactly what I had experienced. That level of efficiency was truly revolutionary.

With each group being trained, we discussed why the video lectures were so much shorter than live lectures. There were basically four reasons.[32]

---

32 4 Reasons: Why are video lectures are shorter than live lectures?. Retrieved from http://schooled.lodgemccammon.com

When lecturing to a video camera in a quiet room, there are no interruptions, fewer tangents, less repetition of content for a student who was not listening, and there is no need to reteach yesterday's lesson if you feel like students did not understand it (there's already a video for it!). In the classroom, interruptions, tangents, repetition, and re-teaching eat up almost all the class time. These teachers appreciated, like Katie and I did, the opportunity to efficiently record their content and then have students click play instead of repeating themselves. This led to our catch phrase for the training: "Life's too short. Stop repeating yourself. Flip your classroom."

On the last day of training, each teacher was required to create a "Why I Flipped My Classroom" video.[33] This was the best way for us to know if they learned what we wanted them to learn. It was also a great way for them to communicate with students, parents, administrators and peers on why they decided to make this change in their teaching. Once they completed this final video, they received a certificate and were asked to fill out a survey about the training.

The most common feedback we received from the survey was that the participants wished that this program had been required during their pre-service teacher training at their college or university before they became a teacher. I could not have agreed more with this sentiment. If I had learned how to solve the problem of time at Maryville College or the University of Tennessee before I entered the classroom, I would not have failed so epically.

After we trained these 40 teachers, I took all the training materials and put them on a website, offering the flipped classroom training program to anyone for free.[34] I wanted to be sure the resources we created could be used for free by any teacher in the world.

---

33 Exit Interviews. Retrieved from http://schooled.lodgemccammon.com
34 Online Training. Retrieved from http://schooled.lodgemccammon.com

The Flipped Classroom Training Program (For Undergrads)

Based on the feedback from the teachers we trained and because the FI was part of the College of Education at NCSU, I decided that I would use some of the donated money to also create a training program for pre-service teachers (those who were in training programs to be teachers). The first thing I needed to do was to find a "Katie Gimbar" type undergrad who could model this teaching method as a pre-service teacher. I needed someone who was awesome and inspiring. I needed someone that other undergraduates would look up to. To this end, I emailed a few friends and colleagues who taught education classes at NCSU. Their response was unanimous. Assir Abushouk was the guy.[35]

Assir was double majoring in secondary mathematics and statistics. He first went through the teacher training program in person at the FI with the last training cohort, making note of what he thought could be modified for his pre-service peers. I then worked with him to develop materials for a training that could be used at the undergraduate level. I also helped him implement the teaching method while he was student teaching in the fall semester of 2012.[36] After Assir had a chance to experience this method, I helped him record a series of frequently asked question one-take videos, which I folded into the training program to help other pre-service teachers adopt the method.[37]

After the materials were created, we piloted the new training in early 2013 with a group of five pre-service teachers from the College of Education at NCSU.[38] Once that was done, a free training for pre-service teachers was offered online, just like the teacher training.

---

35 Assir's Introduction.
36 Assir Abushouk's Flipped Classroom.
37 Assir's FAQ.
38 Pre-Service Training Overview.
Retrieved from http://schooled.lodgemccammon.com

At this point, I was convinced that this training program would be a fantastic class for undergrads. I had built the pre-service training program in the image of the teacher training program, and it made all the sense in the world to offer it to more students at NCSU. Allowing them to receive course credit for doing the work would be the ideal next step. I gathered the data that I had collected from the trainings and in the summer of 2013 I requested a meeting with the dean of the College of Education. I showed her the curriculum and presented the findings. I suggested that it might be a great class to offer our undergraduates so that they are able to graduate knowing how to solve the problem of time in their future classrooms. I even offered to teach it. For free. (Seriously.)

The dean thought the training was great. She said the data was great. However, she said that I would not be allowed to teach a class in the College of Education. She told me that the faculty (education professors) get together and decide what courses will be offered and who will teach them. Since I was not part of the faculty, and my training and these ideas did not line up with the current goals of their pre-service program, the training would not be included as a course offering.

I was starting to see a pattern. First, I was told that my work did not belong at the FI. Strike one. Now, I was told that my training couldn't be offered as a course to pre-service teachers because my work did not fit with the current goals of the College of Education. This was strange. I had developed a very scalable, easy to understand, and inexpensive method for drastically improving the efficiency of any classroom. I had evidence from real classroom teachers that it worked. The Goodnights had funded the development of a training program around my method. Teachers across the world were now using the free online resources to change the efficiency of their classrooms.[39] Organizations, districts and schools were contacting me to come speak about what I had created. It seemed that the

---

39 Why I Flipped My Classroom – Online Participants. Retrieved from http://schooled.lodgemccammon.com

only people not interested in my solution were the people I worked for at the university. I didn't let it get me down. That was only strike two.

THE FLIPPED CLASSROOM TRAINING PROGRAM (FOR PROFESSORS)

Like the teachers who said that they wished they had this training when they were in school, the undergraduate trainees, when filling out the survey at the end of the training, said they wished their professors used these efficient and active teaching methods in their university classes. All of them acknowledged that most of the class time in college was spent sitting and listening to lectures.

Based on that feedback, I determined that the last piece of this puzzle was to use what was left of the Goodnight's donation to work with a professor at NCSU and develop a "professor" version of our training. None of the education professors I talked to were interested in working with me on this project. In fact, most of them preferred to debate the merits of the method and express how they disagreed with the pedagogy. They said things like, "Students won't be able to learn the content from just watching videos" or "This idea is unfair to students who don't have access to the internet." I had to look elsewhere for my model professor.

Back in 2010 and 2011, I had been asked to do a few presentations for the Distance Education Learning Technology Applications (DELTA) group at NCSU. This department was responsible for organizing professional development sessions for professors and teaching assistants (graduate students who taught courses). During the sessions that I facilitated for DELTA, I modeled my one-take video techniques.

Professors are a very tough audience. Remember that academic discourse I mentioned before? That's what happened. I would model a strategy and then talk about the research foundations. Multiple professors would question my methods, seeming to focus on reasons why they might not work. This was very similar to what teachers did. Teachers would just keep asking questions until you could not answer one of them. Once you conceded with "I don't know the answer to that," they would say, "Yup, that's why this won't work in my classroom." Professors were a little different with their style in that they would straight up tell you that your idea won't work based upon their own experience and research. If you didn't effectively argue your agenda, citing specific research studies, they would say, "I would need to see more research on this before deciding to use it in my classroom." I continued to learn a lot from these questions and comments.

In January 2013, I called up my colleague from DELTA who had booked me for these previous sessions and told her that I was looking for a professor to work with on a flipped classroom training program for higher education. She set up a time to meet with me. I thought this was a little strange. I just wanted the names of some professors who might be interested. But OK, sure. Let's have a meeting.

We met three days later. She kicked off the meeting by explaining how DELTA works with professors on these types of projects. First, they identify funding to pay professors to try new methods. Then, they schedule time to train the professor on the new methods. Next, the professor works with the method for a semester. Finally, someone from DELTA talks with the professor to determine whether this method was worthwhile.

She informed me that, based on this process, we might be able to reach out to a professor in the summer of 2013, train them and have them create one flipped lesson (literally one video). The professor would use that flipped lesson in the fall semester of 2013. Finally, we would reconnect with the professor at the end of the fall semester to see how that single lesson went. At that point, I thanked her for her time and ended the meeting. The DELTA process seemed a little too slow for me, so I went a different direction.

Instead, I reached out to my good friend Dr. Steven Toaddy, who had just been hired by the psychology department at NCSU to recommend curricular changes to undergraduate psychology courses. We discussed the teaching method, piloted 10 flipped lessons in a large enrollment (200+ students) psychology classroom,[40] collected student data, and created a series of training materials (very similar to the teacher and pre-service training programs) that could be used by professors who wanted to learn more about the one-take flipped classroom.[41] We did this over the course of January, February and March in 2013. Like the other two programs, once the training program was complete, I put the materials online and offered it as a free course.

Do you think that the people from DELTA were thrilled about this? No, they were not. They sent an email to my boss reprimanding me for doing this work. Was this strike three? My work does not belong at the FI (strike one), I am not allowed to teach a class for the College of Education or even have my methods included (strike two), and now I am being reprimanded for working with professors on campus. That sounds like a strike three to me, but I also got some confirmation. Soon after my boss received that email from DELTA, I was asked to resign.

That's OK. NCSU is a great place with a lot of fantastic people doing great work. I just didn't fit in.

RESULTS

One goal for creating these training programs was to get more exposure and more speaking engagements. That surely happened. As a result of what I learned from the training, I created hundreds of new videos. Those videos went right into the pipeline on YouTube and received thousands of views. As they received more views, I received more emails about speaking engagements.

---

40 Steven Toaddy's Classroom.
41 Steven's FAQ.
Retrieved from http://schooled.lodgemccammon.com

Another goal was to have a better answer for those who were convinced that this method would not work in their classrooms. Since we were offering free online flipped classroom training, hundreds of excellent teachers across all grade levels and content areas completed our training programs. In addition, the training required teachers to not only record, reflect on, and submit 20 lecture videos, they also had to create a "Why I Flipped My Classroom" video explaining the reasons they decided to use this method.

These videos were a valuable resource when someone would approach us and say something like, "I don't see how this could possibly work in high school English." Now, I could simply send them a list of videos created by one of our high school English training graduates that included a video on why they decided to flip their classroom. That was a more appropriate and helpful response than what I was able to say before, which was, "Do your best adapting Katie's model in your classroom." It only took 10 months and a boatload (a row boat, not a mid-sized ski boat) of money to get there.[42]

One might think that a teacher who asks, "How can this work in my classroom?" is actually interested in wanting to learn more about how it might work. However, that was not always the case. I could now respond to that question by saying something like, "Hey, here are some videos from teachers who teach what you teach and are successfully using the method." More times than not, a skeptical teacher would respond and say, "Well, that's fine for them, but I don't know how it would work in *my* classroom, with *my* kids and at *my* school."

I recognized that sentiment from my years of work in professional development. I think what these teachers were really trying to say was, "This is not what I currently do in my classroom. The way I currently teach is my superhero power." I absolutely get it. I had those same thoughts

---

42 Training Results. Retrieved from http://schooled.lodgemccammon.com

throughout all my teacher training and during professional development sessions I attended when I was a teacher. I had no interest in listening to the ideas of others; I was only interested in doing what I was currently doing, promoting my own agenda.

But, you know what? Despite some of the pushback I received, I was thrilled that our training materials were impacting thousands of educators across the world. I was elated to receive tweets, Facebook messages and emails from hundreds of teachers saying that my materials changed their lives. Many said that solving the problem of time drastically increased their job satisfaction. Some said they went from feeling burnt out to being excited about teaching again. I couldn't help but be reminded yet again of my time as the head of the sunshine committee. I was making lives better in schools across the world.

CHAPTER 16

I Don't Lecture

• • •

SPEAKING OF EDUCATORS APPROACHING ME and questioning how this could work for them, the most confounding and fascinating response I have heard from a teacher is, "That would not work for my classroom because I don't lecture." Now, I am certainly open to the notion that some teachers have figured out how to teach without needing an abundance of lecture, but I was curious to know more about those who said they "don't lecture at all." How did they do it? I had (and still have) never been in a classroom where the teacher did not lecture, even just a little. I have never been in a classroom where the teacher did not have information they were responsible for transmitting to their students.

The first few times I heard this statement I replied by saying, "That's great! Can I come observe your classroom to see how you are teaching without lecture?" Most of the teachers would immediately say yes, but then would not follow up to schedule a time for me to visit their classroom. I did not automatically assume that it was because they didn't want me to observe, but it did make me suspicious. However, a number of them did allow me to come in. When I observed these "no lecture" classrooms, for the most part, I saw the same thing. It was amazing. I sat in the back of the classroom and watched the teacher start the lesson with an assessment then lecture for most of the class period, and finish by giving the students a worksheet-type assignment. This looked very familiar.

You may be thinking, "If they were lying, why would they let you come into their classroom and observe?" I was thinking the same thing. But, observing this was not the most fascinating part, it was the discussion with the teacher after the class was over that provided the bombshell. To help illustrate, I will give you a representative example. I observed a high school science classroom led by a teacher who told me he did not lecture. I sat through his 45-minute lecture on atoms. The students left, and I asked him how he thought the lesson went. He said it went well. I asked him if that's the structure of his normal classes. He said it was. Then, I asked if he could describe the activities I had seen over this 60-minute class period. He said that he had started with a formative assessment. Then, he provided some direct instruction, where he talked about the content and asked questions in order to provide some context for the students to apply their understanding of the content.

Wow. So, he doesn't lecture, he uses "direct instruction," which means that he stands in front of students and delivers information. For years, education leaders have been telling teachers to stop lecturing because it's an ineffective method for delivering content and it takes up too much class time. Lecture has been demonized. Well, let's be perfectly clear. The *word* lecture has become demonized. If leaders are talking about how lecture is terrible, but don't provide a practical alternative that meets the same goal as lecture, then this results in only the word being terrible. Clearly, people are still going to use the practice.

This teacher had not changed a thing about his teaching method except for the words he uses to describe it. I saw this (and continue to see it) over and over again across grade levels and content areas. I visited an elementary classroom and saw the same thing. Less time was spent on lecture than in a high school class, but there was still some amount of lecture and this time the teacher called it "modeling." I visited a middle school English class and saw the same thing. Again, the teacher spent more than half the period lecturing to the students and called it "discussion." Lecture is bad (apparently), so teachers are changing the *name* of it instead of changing what they are doing. That's genius. It really is. It's such an amazing survival mechanism.[43]

This practice of renaming strategies instead of actually changing practice has been a common occurrence in our education system since the beginning. Education leaders have been giving lectures (yes, lectures) about a need for more active classrooms for decades. According to research, if students do almost anything other than sit and listen to lectures for most of the class period, achievement will increase. This is not shocking.

For decades, instead of solving the problem of time, which keeps most teachers from creating active learning environments, we rename strategies to try to get around the real problem, making it seem like change is happening. It's the old smoke and mirrors technique.

Over the years, we've renamed active learning many things including project-based learning, inquiry and discovery. However, despite having subtle differences in their approach or technique, these are all terms that imply active learning. Meanwhile, we're saying "lecture is bad," and because we don't know how to make a change here, we just rename it "direct instruction." But then, we say direct instruction is bad, so we rename it "modeling." This seems to apply to other teaching strategies as well. Everyone talked about the importance of "personalized instruction," but it didn't appear to be leveraged by all teachers, so we renamed it "differentiated instruction." When that didn't catch on, we renamed it again, referring to it as "Universal Design for Learning." We have even renamed the concept of rigor (the level of challenge an assignment provides a student). I think we are supposed to call that "grit" now. The renaming goes on and on while what happens day-to-day in classrooms stays the same.

---

43   Teachers Are Going to Lecture. Retrieved from
http://schooled.lodgemccammon.com

I sat in classrooms observing teachers who told me they used inquiry instead of lecture. I sat there for an hour and watched traditional lecture-based teaching practices. I observed classrooms that were using project-based learning, where the teachers told me that letting students do a worksheet after the lecture was a "project." In turn, we have created a culture where using the most current buzzwords to describe teaching is the same thing as making a change to instruction.

The fact remains that lecture (or whatever you would like to call it) is gobbling up most of the instructional time in classrooms. This is the main reason why teachers don't have time to create active learning environments (or whatever we are calling them this year). It's also why we don't have time to personalize learning (or whatever we are calling it now).

Now that I had a solid grip on my solution to the problem of time and had grown a small audience, I left the FI in 2013 and struck out on my own. My business model didn't change. I wanted to continue to publish free resources that helped teachers solve the problem of time while facilitating presentations, workshops and keynote speeches.

CHAPTER 17

The McCammon Method

• • •

I HAVE VIDEOS THAT ANSWER all the frequently asked questions. I have a small bit of research connecting this method to education "best practices." I have worked with every kind of teacher across every grade level, content area, and across the world. You would think that level of detail and accompanying resources would be enough for educators to get on board.

Nope. The next common response from teachers arose. "Flipping the classroom won't work for me because I don't know what to do with my class time." Huh. My initial response was, "Do whatever you want. Try things. Experiment. Innovate. Anything you do that gets the students active in the learning process is better than just lecturing." I was growing weary of these questions. I felt I had gone above and beyond in providing resources, guidance, advice and training that made up a scalable and simple solution to the biggest problem in our education system, and now people are just picking at the details.

Of course, I am being slightly hyperbolic. I actually found all of this quite fascinating, especially the parts that didn't make sense to me. I found the notion of people being worried about having *too much* extra class time bizarre. If that became a problem for every teacher in the U.S., I think it would be the best problem that has ever existed!

Having teachers voice their concerns about what to do with class time allowed me the opportunity to continue to broaden my own perspective on best practices in teaching. Of course, my first response was, "Use music in the classroom and have students create one-take videos!" But I wanted to go a step further and outline what strategies every teacher could do every day if they had time. In a way, I wanted to establish my own professional teaching standard. So, I went in search of the most simple and powerful strategies that could be implemented by any teacher to drastically improve the learning environment. I identified two strategies that teachers could use to challenge students every day: have students teach[44] and get students moving. [45]

OK, try this one for size. Every student should record and publish a concise one-take video about each topic they have learned. The assignment would be to re-teach each lesson. This would be real student accountability. If you want to know if a student is learning, if they are doing their job, just pull up their playlist on YouTube and watch them teach and explain their version of every lesson. This would not only make each student completely accountable for their learning, but I know that teaching can be a rigorous form of learning.[46]

Also, every student, at any age, can benefit from kinesthetic (movement-based) activities. In fact, brain research supports lots of links between movement and learning. For example, that pesky oxygen is essential for a brain to function, and enhanced blood flow increases the amount of oxygen transported to the brain. Sitting passively limits the blood flow to the brain, hence limiting the brain's optimal functioning. Physical activity is a great way to increase blood flow, and hence oxygen, to the brain. Also, there is a correlation between movement and attention. If students are

---

44 Education's New Video Accountability Model.
45 Balance.
46 When Students Become Teachers.
Retrieved from http://schooled.lodgemccammon.com

active in their learning, they are more attentive to the task at hand, as opposed to sitting passively with their mind wandering during a lecture. In addition, many studies connect movement to increased cognition, better memory, reduced likelihood of depression, improved classroom behavior and increased academic performance.[47] In fact, take a moment to get up and move before continuing to read. Take a short walk and get that blood flowing.

Now, all I needed to do was take all these strategies and design a simple and scalable teaching method that teachers could use every day to enhance lecture-based classrooms. Thus, The McCammon Method (I know, eye roll, I named it after myself) of teaching leverages three simple and powerful research-based instructional strategies.[48]

1. All my lectures are recorded and published, creating a self-paced learning resource for my students. They can watch my one-take lecture videos anywhere, any time and as many times as they need in order to process the information.
2. Throughout every lesson, I challenge my students to work in groups to re-teach the content, assigning them to create, review and reflect on one-take lecture or paperslide videos.
3. I take every opportunity throughout each lesson to get students out of their seats, up and moving. Movement increases blood flow to the brain and can promote attention, memory and creative thinking.

How cool and simple is that?

Let's recap. I solved the problem of time. I answered all the questions associated with one-take video creation. I created a training program,

---

47 Kinesthetic Research.
48 The McCammon Method.
Retrieved from http://schooled.lodgemccammon.com

helping thousands of teachers use the videos to enhance their classrooms. I even provided practical suggestions, resources and research on best practices for what to do with the class time. So, we're done, right? Problem solved. The story is over. I have come to the end, and I can move on to something else now? Nope.

It turns out that time was not the biggest problem all along. I had helped lots of teachers make this transition and change what happens in their classrooms, but I didn't see a massive push of all educators getting on board with this change. Time certainly is a problem, and a big one, but it's not the main one we face.

CHAPTER 18

Policy to Incentivize Change

• • •

RELUCTANCE TO CHANGE SEEMS TO be the biggest problem in education and I feared that education only changes when forced to do so. I believed passionately that I had a solution. I also believed that I had done my due diligence to show that the solution was scalable and would result in a massive improvement to our education system if implemented on a large scale. Thus, while I was developing all these teaching resources, I also started dabbling in the concept of designing policies that would incentivize teachers to make this change.

At this point, many teachers would stand up and cheer, "Yes. We need policies that pay teachers more for doing this job!" Well, that's not exactly what I am saying. Simply paying the existing teachers more for what they are currently doing may not be the answer. Logically, that will only further incentivize them to continue doing exactly what they are doing.

MY FIRST POLICY IDEA

At the end of 2011, I wrote another op-ed for the News & Observer suggesting that we should pay teachers per pupil and design specialized training programs (like the free training I created) that prepare teachers to excel in handling larger numbers of students. One of the findings from the data we collected from the teachers who went through the flipped classroom training program was that, because they became more efficient with their practice, they were able to successfully teach their larger classes. Paying teachers per pupil seems like the most logical, simple and quantifiable merit pay policy that could be implemented at the school or district level. Once teachers completed training and demonstrated that they could handle the larger classes without decreasing the quality of education for their students, they should receive an increase in salary. For example, if a teacher takes on 30 percent more students, then he or she would receive a 30 percent increase in pay. It's that simple.

If you're thinking "Lodge, it's 2011. No one is reading op-eds in newspapers," you're wrong. There was a small amount of local backlash from my article. Some people became downright angry at me and my idea and felt compelled to share. I received some emails from these lovely fans. One lady, who was on a school board, approached me in the grocery store one afternoon, got in my face, and said, "I can't believe you want to fire teachers." I replied by saying, "Technically, if teachers are willing and able, after being trained of course, to teach larger class sizes or additional classes, then we would need fewer teachers. However, I never said anything in the article about firing teachers. It would just be an efficient solution as the population grows." She stormed off, seemingly not interested in having a conversation about it. She just wanted to be angry and complain. Was that the kind of person we needed on the school board? It remains to be seen.

The following school year I heard about a few high schools in North Carolina that were allowing teachers to give up their planning period in order to teach an additional class every day, for additional pay. This school-level policy was met with some criticism. The fear was that the teachers would be offering a lower quality education if they took on more students. To my knowledge, there was no training requirement before allowing a teacher to opt into this initiative. Without being trained on how to be more efficient, taking on more students certainly may decrease the quality of instruction.

I believe these schools missed the opportunity to promote change. Any time there is an economic incentive to dangle (e.g., more pay, better working conditions), that incentive can be used to get employees to go through additional trainings in order to qualify to receive the incentive. The teaching workforce is no different, but I rarely (basically never) see the industry take advantage of this simple economic principle.

My Second Policy Idea

In August 2012, I was invited to attend a VIP dinner after a keynote speech I gave at a regional education conference. I showed up wearing jeans, a Nintendo t-shirt and tennis shoes. Unbeknownst to me, the dinner was in a private room at a fancy restaurant. Between you, me and the jumbo shrimp, even if I knew this, I still would have worn the same outfit. There are benefits to being a musician. One is that nobody ever expects you to dress up. In fact, they often expect me *not* to dress up for this type of occasion, so they can say something like, "Oh, look at the artist over there with the messy hair who does not know how to dress himself."

At any rate, I sat down to eat with a group of school leaders, business people and education professors from the area – the VIPs. As is the norm in these situations, the conversation quickly shifted from pleasantries to education. And because the topic was education, most of them were just complaining and describing the problems. The school leaders complained that the pre-service teachers coming out of the colleges and universities were not prepared for the teaching positions, and more than half were quitting before making it to five years. The business people were complaining that students coming out of high schools and colleges did not have the critical thinking and communication skills necessary to thrive in the workplace. The professors said that they were doing a great job training pre-service teachers, but that the rigors and regulations from the school districts don't allow for new teachers to fully utilize the research-based skills and theories they learn at the colleges and universities.

This turned into an argument of sorts, each group blaming the other groups for the system not working very well. Each perspective shared was accompanied by a platitude like, "Schools just need to spend more time on critical thinking and communication skills so when students enter the workforce they will be prepared."

As the conversation moved forward, I took out a small notebook and a pen, and began taking notes on what they were talking about. About 15 minutes into my note taking, I realized that everyone was just describing the problem in a way that made sure they were not in any way culpable. Each group was saying that change needed to happen, but that they were not responsible for making changes. That's typical.

After a few more minutes, there was a pause in the conversation, so I spoke up. "May I offer a perspective?" Of course, they all said, "yes."

"It sounds like we all want changes in education." I looked around the room and they were all nodding, so I continued. "At the fundamental level, we want changes in the day-to-day activities that happen in the classrooms, to prepare students to be thinkers and communicators. I am sitting here listening to everyone use platitudes to describe the problems, but I don't hear any solutions. So, I would like to propose one."

"The overarching problem I hear is that nobody knows who is responsible for making significant changes to the school system, or even if changes can be made. If you want an answer for that, I will provide one. Do you want one?"

At this point I had stood up and was looking around the table, looking everyone in the face to see their response to this question. Most people were nodding, some said yes out loud. I continued.

"The districts or counties in every state that have the best schools are the ones best positioned for making any type of changes in the education system overall. I am talking about schools that offer the best working conditions, 'best' students, and highest pay. In North Carolina, for example, those might be Wake, Guilford and Charlotte-Mecklenburg counties. Most of the students coming out of education schools in North Carolina want to get a job in one of those three school districts. In addition, many teachers in North Carolina schools (not in those three counties) would like to work in Wake, Guilford, and Charlotte-Mecklenburg. Finally, many teachers from outside the state who are looking for a North Carolina teaching job (like I did) want one in Wake, Guilford, or Charlotte-Mecklenburg. For every open position in the best schools in North Carolina, there are many applicants. Therein lies the opportunity for the best schools to create policies that will cause a significant change in the education system. Get it?"

I looked around the room again and I saw a series of puzzled looks, so I continued to explain.

"If the three most sought after counties in North Carolina got together and designed, say an 80-hour online training that everyone who wanted a job there would need to complete, that would cause a spark. The best counties would basically be establishing a professional teaching standard for the state. Let's say that this training requires teachers to learn how to free-up class time by recording and publishing their lessons, making their content delivery efficient and self-paced."

I scanned the room again and I saw some people nodding. This was what I just spoke about during my keynote, so the information was not new. I was on a roll.

"Once this training is established, every teacher who wants a job in one of the three most desired counties would have to complete it before even applying. Most of the candidates coming out of the colleges and universities would be willing to complete the training in hopes of getting one of the best jobs in the state. Many teachers from other school districts would be willing to do that as well. Even teachers from out of state would likely be willing to spend 80 hours to have a shot at the best jobs."

"But the real magic here is that these districts would be putting a stake in the ground, saying that 'This training is what we think every teacher in North Carolina should do.' It would mean that in the state of North Carolina, teachers don't lecture live. They provide their lecture content to students via video both inside and outside the classroom. This would be an educational revolution that would benefit every student."

I could tell that I had lost a few people at the table, but I felt compelled to push through to the end. I raised my voice and started flailing my arms wildly.

"This, you see, would cause a chain reaction! Pre-service teachers, who are customers of the universities in North Carolina, would demand that this district training be a part of their program at the colleges and universities. Thus, these three counties could successfully dictate that new methods be integrated at the pre-service training level. This means that all pre-service teachers would eventually receive this training, not just the ones who want to work in the big three counties. So, students who are trained in North Carolina's new professional teaching standard would go to work in schools across the state. Then, it's just a waiting game. After about a decade, the scales would tip, and we would have a critical mass of teachers in every school across the state who are adhering to North Carolina's new professional teaching standard."

"Because this professional teaching standard ensures that North Carolina would be moving toward having the most transparent and efficient education system in the country, we could then allow teachers to opt into larger class sizes in order to receive higher pay."

At this point, everyone looked confused, except some of the professors, who were scowling. I understood why. Remember, I had wanted these strategies integrated at the College of Education at NCSU, and I was told that they would not be allowed because they didn't align with current goals. This plan was really a way to force universities to change the way they train teachers, and it turns out that professors are as averse to change as the rest of us. Needless to say, they were not happy about this plan.

Many others seemed lost by my idea, so I said that I would create a one-take video of the concept and share it with them, so they could watch it as many times as necessary to process the information. I sat back down and continued eating.

No one really had anything to say in response. It was quiet for about 30 seconds and then the conversation picked back up with the same people describing the same problems as before. The complaining continued, with no solutions being offered. I just shrugged my shoulders and whispered to a principal sitting next to me, "I guess nobody wants to talk about solutions." He responded by saying, "I don't think anyone followed what you were even talking about."

I did, in fact, record a video of my idea and sent it to everyone at the VIP dinner.[49] The only person that responded was one of the assistant superintendents. She wrote, "I understand what you are saying, but you are going to have a hard time getting people on board with this idea because it will cause too much change. You mentioned that it seemed like people only want to complain about the problems and not solve them. Actually,

---

49 Leveraging Incentives. Retrieved from http://schooled.lodgemccammon.com

people just want to do all they can to keep their jobs. Complaining about a problem does not fix a problem, but it makes it seem like you are working to fix it if you talk about it all the time. However, fixing a problem means that you don't get to complain about the problem any more. If complaining about the problem was a big part of your job, then your job is in jeopardy. Thanks for sending the video." She was wise.

To my knowledge, the school leaders in the group did not use my plan to help change education in their states. But, I maintain that the responsibility for making change rests on the ability of the best school districts to leverage incentives to spark a chain reaction.

My Third Policy Idea

In the fall semester of 2013, I was hired to facilitate a series of workshops for Beaufort County Schools in North Carolina on the one-take flipped classroom. Mr. Cole, the 2013 North Carolina Principal of the Year, attended one of these workshops. The day he attended, the workshop ended at 3 p.m. and he was slated to speak to the participants from 3-3:30 p.m. Basically, he told them that education policies were going to change in the state, and if any of the teachers wanted to weigh in regarding merit pay, salaries or things along those lines, then they should email him their ideas. He said he would then take all those ideas and present them to a committee that was advising the governor.

After Mr. Cole finished presenting, I sheepishly approached him and asked if I could send him a proposal. He told me that he'd be thrilled to hear my thoughts and told me to pass them along. Sweet.

The governor was looking for ideas around an alternative pay scale for teachers that didn't simply reward them for every additional year they stayed in the profession. I assumed that they were interested in what looked more like a merit pay system. Merit pay means that teachers would be eligible for higher salaries based on their demonstrated mastery of skills. This is a tough sell because there really is no professional standard for teachers. The question becomes "How do you create a merit pay system when it's unclear what every teacher is required to do every day?" First, there needs to be a professional standard for what it means to be a teacher in North Carolina. Only then, will we be able to design a merit pay system to reward teachers for excelling at those professional standards.

I tackled this challenge with an excited energy, putting together a document called the NC 60/30/10 Plan.[50] This was the first real policy proposal I had ever written, and boy did it go off the rails in a big way.

In the NC 60/30/10 Plan, there were three possible teacher "levels" and corresponding salaries for educators in North Carolina. You can be an Apprentice, Master, or Career teacher. Apprentice teachers would make $32,000 and would make up about 60 percent of the teacher workforce. Master teachers would make $52,000. To be considered for a Master position, a teacher would need to have completed a training where they record and publish their lecture content along with receiving high marks on evaluations and other professional assessments. Only 30 percent of teachers would be at the Master level. Finally, the remaining 10 percent of teachers would be at the Career level. These teachers would make $72,000. Master teachers would have the opportunity to move up to Career status if they successfully earned a master's degree or Ph.D. Evaluations and other professional assessments would help determine who would get Career positions.

In 2013, the top salary for a teacher in North Carolina was around $50,000, based on 25 years of experience. In our plan, a teacher could make $52,000 in just a few years if they recorded their lecture content, solving the problem of time in their classroom. They would have a chance to make $72,000 if they earned an advanced degree. The thought was that

---

50 NC 60/30/10 Plan. Retrieved from http://schooled.lodgemccammon.com

if teachers had the possibility to make $72,000 within five years of service, it could end any type of teacher shortage. There would be a massive influx of new teacher talent given those incentives. It would draw some of the best and brightest into the teaching workforce.

In addition, based on the current education budget in 2013, this plan would reduce teacher salary expenditures by about 10 percent. Most of the teacher workforce would be making $32,000 (starting salary for North Carolina teachers was $30,800 in 2013) and only a small percentage would be making $52,000 or $72,000. I thought it was brilliant.

There were more details included in this plan, but the idea was that it would require any teacher who wanted to move past the $32,000 Apprentice level to successfully complete a version of the free training that I had developed and piloted at the FI.

This plan was also a move toward creating a professional teaching standard. It would help outline what every North Carolina teacher should do every day. Every teacher would either be working toward or already have all their lecture content recorded and available as a self-paced resource for their students and parents.

I sent my plan off to Mr. Cole, who responded to my email a few hours later saying that he read the document and thought it was interesting. He also mentioned that he would keep it in mind when he had discussions with the committee. I thought that response was good. I considered it a solid use of the time that it took to write it. Honestly, I didn't really expect anything to happen. I mean, I am not a policy person and I assumed my simplistic, agenda-driven document wouldn't be considered as anything other than a simplistic opinion.

The next day, Mr. Cole sent me another email that included some text from a discussion forum. It turned out that he shared my document with some other education leaders in Beaufort County and requested feedback. Uh-oh. My immediate feeling was that of discomfort. It was my understanding that he would be taking a handful of ideas to the committee and discussing them. I didn't know that he was going to share my document publicly. However, in all fairness, I did email this document without making any requests or stipulations that it be kept private. After a few more minutes of thought, I decided that it was good that he considered my document interesting enough to share with a wider audience. I certainly wanted it to spark conversation, and that it did.

I read a few of the responses from the discussion forum and they were mostly skeptical regarding the plausibility of the plan. I agreed with most of their comments and I didn't really have the answers to their questions or criticisms. Again, I was not a policy person. For example, some were asking how this might impact teacher retirement. Others were critical, stating that this would create more work for school leadership because decisions would have to be made to determine which teachers would be promoted.

One thing that disappointed me was that exactly none of the discussion was around the merits of the training requirement and how it would lead to the creation of a real professional teaching standard for North Carolina teachers. The whole purpose of me writing the plan was to get people talking about how a required training could create standards for our education system. The feedback made me realize that the scope of the plan was too broad and that everyone was getting caught up in how this would impact their job, not thinking about the broader day-to-day classroom implications. That was my mistake. I was learning.

The day after I received the email from Mr. Cole with the feedback, I received another email. This one was from a NC Policy Watch reporter. The reporter was writing because she "had a few questions about the NC 60/30/10 Plan." Wait, what?

I didn't respond right away because I was facilitating a training, but I thought it was interesting that a reporter found, and was interested in discussing, the plan. That afternoon when my session ended, I had some time to reply. Before I started writing the email, I went on NC Policy Watch's website to learn more about what they do. I saw that they were a policy watchdog group, of sorts. I clicked around a bit and ended up on their Facebook page. I wanted to see what type of work they shared and how many people followed their work. Low and behold, the most recent post on Facebook was a link to an article about my plan.

The article stated that the reporter had attempted to get in touch with the author of the plan (me), but that I had not responded. It went on to say that this plan was currently being considered by the general assembly for how to change the teacher pay scale in North Carolina. My first thought was, "Wow. That's absolutely not true." My second thought was, "Wow. If that is true, that's pretty interesting." My third thought was, "Good grief. I wish I hadn't put my name on it."

I was proud of the plan, but if you read it with the context of "the general assembly is currently considering this plan as a possible change in education policy for the state" (which, to be clear, it wasn't being considered) it would seem a little silly. The state's education policy was very complex. My plan was very simple. Again, it was about how to get teachers to do this training program to solve the problem of time, increase active learning in classrooms, and create a professional standard. The other details of the plan were grossly generalized and honestly nonsensical when it came to how changes would actually be implemented. I was just an informed citizen with an idea.

The rest of the article was filled with inflammatory reporting language that is common nowadays (using statements like "we uncovered a hidden plan" or "you will never believe what is happening") along with a very poor summary of the plan and a little bit about the author (me). The article even included a music video that I had created for a song I wrote about the state of North Carolina. All in all, it seemed very odd. And not positive.

I figured, "What the heck, I'll reach out to this reporter and see what the deal is with this article." I called her, and we chatted for about 20 minutes. I informed her that, to my knowledge, the general assembly is *not* considering this plan and it was created as a brainstorming document and sent to Mr. Cole with the sole purpose of being added to a pile of other ideas to be pitched to a committee for the governor. She simply did not believe me. She asked me questions as if I was part of a conspiracy to destroy education in North Carolina.

It was an extremely unusual and somewhat humorous conversation. She kept asking me whom I was really working for and if the governor had contracted with me to design this plan. I am pretty sure that I laughed a few times before answering these questions with a, "What? No." The conversation ended abruptly with the call being "disconnected" in the middle of something I was saying. That is what she said when she emailed me back later to tell me that she would publish a follow-up article about what we had discussed.

All I could think was that this was some strange and inappropriate reporting. I knew that this kind of thing went on all the time, with some reporters just making things up to shock people and increase readership, but I had never been the target of it before. I didn't take it too personally. But then, it got a little out of control.

A few hours after my phone conversation with the reporter, Diane Ravitch blogged about the reporter's article and my plan. I had no idea who she was at the time, but I quickly came to find out that she was an author focused on educational issues. I also realized that she had a rather large number of people, interested in educational issues, who read her blog and social media posts. It seemed that her "contribution" was to fan the flames of said issues to incite outrage.

Ravitch's blog post, "Greatest Insult to Teachers Ever Cooked Up," and associated social media statements were a call to action to stop what she considered to be the most egregious affront to public school education ever considered in North Carolina. She praised the reporter from NC Policy Watch for uncovering this scandal and expressed her outrage that the general assembly was considering this new legislation.

Ravitch called on people across the country to speak out against it. She provided her own (inaccurate and misleading) summary of the NC 60/30/10 Plan and then linked to the actual document. Her statement was largely incendiary and inflammatory, seemingly written so that people would get angry. Yet again, there was little or no attention paid to the most important details of the plan: how it would solve the problem of time and help establish a professional standard for teachers.

Unlike the impact of the article written by NC Policy Watch (it resulted in a handful of negative comments), Ravitch's blog post started a brushfire of negativity. There were hundreds of comments and tweets in response to her call for action. Many of them stated a disapproval of the plan for one reason or another. Another batch went into great detail about how the plan was terrible and how it would never work. However, the most bizarre series of comments were personal attacks directed at me. Anonymous angry people were saying that I didn't know anything about education, that I was just another ignorant policymaker trying to make money from the education system. That I was an idiot. There were so many of these that I had to stop reading. In the middle of this maelstrom, a friend emailed me and said, "Don't read the comments. There be dragons there." Many more mean comments rolled in. I didn't really have much experience with this type of negativity, though I knew that it happened all the time to politicians and celebrities.

Not only were there possibly thousands of people speaking out against my plan, I also now considered this idea to be a complete failure. Virtually none of them were talking about the merits of using incentives to train teachers to solve the problem of time. They were just spewing anger about how much they hated change, or me, and then some of them would transition into talking about their personal agendas.

A few hours later, the emails started. I received more than 100 nasty emails in the first 24 hours. People were personally offended by my plan and wanted to write me a little letter to tell me so. I was called an idiot, fool, fraud, moron, and other less kind insults. People wrote that they hated my work, that they hated me personally, that they would do everything they could to make sure that I would never work again. People wrote and told me that I was a terrible musician. People wrote and said that I was a bad dancer. You be the judge.[51]

The emails that really upset me were the messages that referenced my niece, my sister's daughter. I write and record music with her and post the video products on YouTube. One fan wrote about how they hoped she does not want to be a teacher because I will have ruined that for her. Another stated that they hoped she has terrible teachers, so she grows up to be as stupid as her uncle. So, things were not going great.

In full disclosure, I was nervous about my career as a speaker at this point. I had just recently left the FI and was leaning heavily on my reputation and online resources to perpetuate my work. Having thousands of nasty comments, tweets and a few blog posts painting me in gross colors, would not help that cause. But the other real impact I noticed was that I was receiving thousands of hits on my website and thousands of views on my videos. I thought, wow, maybe the old saying is true. Maybe there is no such thing as bad publicity.

---

51 Lindy Hop and Charleston. Retrieved from http://schooled.lodgemccammon.com

Three days later, the comments, tweets, Facebook posts and emails stopped. The angry horde seemed to have moved on to burn the next village.

Side note: The only negative outcome related to my work came almost a year later. I was asked to give the opening keynote speech at the Pennsylvania Educational Technology Expo and Conference in Hershey, Pennsylvania. My picture and biography were published on their website and social media announcements were made about my participation. About a month before the conference, 11 months after the NC 60/30/10 Plan was talked about briefly in social media by Ravitch and others, the organizers cut me from the program stating that I would be "too controversial."

Fear not, dear readers. There was a silver lining other than website hits and video views. A week after this madness, I was asked to have a phone call with the Governor's Education Advisor, Eric Guckian, about my plan and the controversy. Of course, I accepted. The whole point of the exercise was to learn more about education policy and this seemed like an ideal opportunity. It also reminded me to be careful what you wish for, because you just might get it.

I remember getting on the phone with Eric and the first thing he said was, "Hey Lodge, how are you doing?" I responded, "Well, according to the internet, I am the worst person ever." He laughed and said, "Welcome to the club." Politicians experience this every day. It's a tightrope walk where every single decision they make results in countless people screaming (tweeting, Facebooking, etc.) at the top of their lungs about how it's the worst thing that has ever happened. I had received only a tiny dose.

The rest of the conversation was fascinating. Eric spent most of the call talking about the governor's ideas regarding changing teacher pay in North Carolina. He said that requiring a specialized training and creating a professional standard for teachers was a great goal. Thus, he asked if I would work on another plan that connected some of the governor's ideas with mine. I agreed but asked, in jest (sort of), that my name be kept off any document related to this issue. He laughed and then we finished our call.

Upon Eric's request, I created another proposed plan called, "NC Teacher Development Levels," and sent it to the governor's office.[52] A few months later the new teacher salary plan was announced. It was very similar to what I had worked on, except that it did not include any specialized training requirements. This had all been quite interesting, but overall, I thought my involvement was a failure because the new salary plan left out any additional required training that would have solved the problem of time and created a professional teaching standard. The incentives were not utilized to spark any type of real change.

---

52 NC Teacher Development Levels. Retrieved from
http://schooled.lodgemccammon.com

CHAPTER 19

Just Say the Right Words

• • •

I STARTED MY TEACHING CAREER in 2003, soon after the No Child Left Behind law was put into place. Teachers were "required" to meet new standards for student success. We were not told how to do this. Teachers were told there would be new tests and that we would "have to" allocate more classroom time to prepare the students for these tests. Being told these things had exactly zero impact on the day-to-day of my classroom. In fact, I was not aware of any teacher in the school that changed their classroom practice as a result of the No Child Left Behind policy. However, what did change was that we all assured each other and the administration that we were "working toward meeting the new requirements established by No Child Left Behind." We changed the language we used to describe our teaching. Does that sound familiar?

Alas, here lies the real impact of this type of education policy. First, we have a new education requirement decided on by politicians. This causes teachers to grumble in the workrooms, hallways and over beers about how the people making decisions about education have no classroom experience, which is largely true. Next, the new requirements are communicated through school leaders to teachers during meetings. Teachers listen to the new requirements and determine what they need to say (not what they need to change) to remain compliant. Multiple policies can be passed down every year, with the same effect.

This mentality has become the norm as new education policies have been put in place over the past two decades. One of the most recent (and controversial) examples was Common Core. This was an expensive new education policy, rolled out in 2009 that slightly changed the order of topics on the pacing guides. It also "required" some teachers to use new pedagogical strategies. Simply put, many of those selling Common Core not only exclaimed, "Hey, here is the content you are going to cover this year in math." They also said, "We want you to change the way you teach it."

The new method of teaching they promoted was called "discovery." This meant that a teacher would set up a learning environment where students were given time to manipulate information in order to discover their own learning. Hold on now, "discovery" sounds a lot like "inquiry." Which sounds a lot like project-based learning. And they all sound a lot like active learning. Similarly, some proponents of Common Core said, "If you need to tell students information, use 'modeling.'" That's where a teacher stands in front of students and talks about the content. Well, modeling sounds an awful lot like "direct instruction," which is really just lecture.

Here we go again. Common Core was the latest attempt at renaming active learning and lecture. It was the latest attempt at creating a policy that would get students to be hands-on with learning rather than listening to lectures all day in the classroom. What this policy did not address, however, was the problem of time. In fact, it was just something else they "required" teachers to do. Without solving the problem of time, most teachers just kept using their default setting of figuring out what language they needed to use in order to avoid being hassled.

The only teachers I saw who made an easy transition to using some Common Core activities were those who had been through my flipped classroom training. They were able to experiment with the Common Core requirements right away because they had extra classroom time. These teachers had all their lectures published online, so that the students would still be able to access the core content whenever and wherever they needed. Many of the other teachers I talked to over beers rolled their eyes and said, "There will be a different requirement next year. There is no reason to do anything with this Common Core nonsense." Though, these same teachers said that they were adopting Common Core, when asked by their administration.

And this continues.

Social Desirability Bias

This past semester I was having (a few) beers with a middle school science teacher named Amanda, and she was expressing her dissatisfaction regarding the amount of content she was required to deliver to students over the course of a year. She exclaimed, "What they expect me to cover and for students to learn is just too darn much." I responded by asking her what a typical 45-minute class period looks like. She said that the students come in, sit down and take a formative assessment like a quiz on yesterday's lesson. This takes about 10 minutes. Then, she lectures on some new information. This typically takes about 30 minutes. In the last five minutes of class, she has the students complete a worksheet or bookwork to reinforce the new information. She gets through the content by spending about 67 percent of her time on lecture, 22 percent on formative assessment and 11 percent on worksheets.

Amanda was complaining that she didn't have enough time to cover all the required content. I had a solution for her. I said, "If you video record your content, the videos can be 60 to 80 percent shorter than if you present the same information live in the classroom. Doing this will allow you to get through all of your content efficiently." Boom goes the dynamite. That's a clear and simple solution.

She replied, "I am interested in technology and innovation, but I don't want to make any changes to my current teaching methods. What I do in my classroom works for my students."

Isn't that fascinating? She was complaining, straight out, that her current methodologies were *not* working. However, when confronted with a solution to her problem, she was not interested. In fact, she was dismissive. She didn't want a solution, she likely just wanted to describe and complain about the problem.

Amanda's social desirability bias[53] made her say, "I am interested in technology and innovation," but the truth came tumbling out (likely because of the beer) immediately after when she said, "I don't want to make any changes." I am sure that she has sat through meetings and conferences where leaders expressed platitudes like, "teachers need to be open to new ideas" or "students deserve innovative classrooms" or even "teachers who use technology every day are superheroes." Thus, society wants her to say that she is open to all those things. So, Amanda says the right words, but that does not mean that she is going to change. This creates a very tricky situation.

---

53 This is a term from social psychology that describes the tendency of people to answer questions in a way they think others would want to hear, such that they will be viewed favorably by others.

CHAPTER 20

Chipping Away at the Real Problem

• • •

LET'S REVISIT OUR ORIGINAL PROBLEM. How do we create active learning environments for all students? When I started teaching, I thought that we needed more teachers to have personalities like the heroic educators of my childhood; therefore, I tried to solve the problem by trying to emulate those teachers. Next, I was convinced that my music-based teaching method was the solution. A little while later, I was going around telling people that teachers should use one-take video strategies to engage students. Shortly after that, I realized that most teachers don't have time to implement new strategies in their classrooms. That led me to solving the problem of time, because time is what teachers needed in order to start addressing the question of how to create active learning environments.

I have spent over a decade traveling around the country discussing and modeling innovative teaching strategies. I have done work for companies like Microsoft, Siemens, and Discovery Education. I have given keynote speeches at events like the Midwest Education Technology Conference, Gulf Regional Innovative Teaching Conference, and the University of the West Indies Open Lecture.[54] I have observed hundreds of classrooms and had meaningful and (occasionally brutally) honest conversations with scores of teachers, sometimes over beers. I have built free training

---

54 Speeches/Workshops. Retrieved from http://schooled.lodgemccammon.com

programs and collected feedback from teachers across the world. What has all this taught me? Well, I now know that the biggest problem is that many educators are not interested in making changes to their practice, regardless of the benefits.

In my experience, when presented with a new idea, many teachers who claim that they are open to change will respond in one of four ways.

The Questioner: At first, this teacher seems to be interested in change. They tend to ask thoughtful questions like, "Is there research that backs this up?" As the conversation continues and their questions are answered, they ask more questions like, "How would this work in a rural school?" If those questions are also answered, they ask more specific questions like, "How would this work for students who don't speak English because I have three of them this year?" Even if *those* questions are answered, they will continue until they get to a question that is impossible to answer like, "Specifically, how will this work in *my* classroom?" The answer to that question is always, "I'm not sure, because you are not currently using it in your classroom." However, once The Questioner hears that I don't have an answer to any one of his or her questions, they say, "This won't work in my classroom." They did their due diligence by asking questions and determined that it won't work for them. This is one way The Questioner can justify not changing.

The Learner: This teacher seems extremely interested in making changes. They can be seen feverishly jotting down notes during a presentation, filling up page after page in a notebook. They tweet out resources and ideas that are intended to help others make the changes. They return to their schools and share the ideas they gathered with their peers. They love learning about what words to use when having a conversation regarding innovative teaching practices. The Learner is a direct result of social desirability bias. There are many teachers who feel like it's their responsibility to be "in the know" about new strategies and technologies. The

Learner gobbles up all the information in order to make changes to what they know and say, sharing it with others, but is less likely to change to what they do in the classroom.

The Maybe: This teacher seems on the fence about making changes. They say things like, "It makes logical sense to me," and "Maybe I will try it in my classroom." These teachers are generally sold on ideas by seeing strong examples of how changes will benefit their students. Many of The Maybe teachers don't end up adopting new ideas because they leave a presentation, get back to the hustle-bustle of their classroom and never make the time to revisit those ideas they heard about. However, some of The Maybe teachers do follow through and generally do well when changes are made.

The Absolute: This teacher is all about making changes. Like, implement the next day kind of attitude. They say things like, "Holy cow! This solves so many of my problems," or "My students will love this! I need to do it." These teachers are sold on new ideas in a variety of ways (e.g., research, modeling, testimonials), but mostly because they see that it will be a way to better engage students. Most of The Absolute teachers will end up implementing all or at least part of a new idea. While this is great, because of extreme enthusiasm some of them will rush into using the new ideas without fully following the directions or guidelines, which can hinder the effectiveness of the change. The Absolute teachers may even make multiple changes throughout a given year, jumping quickly from one new idea to the next.

In my experience, the majority of the teachers I encounter who claim to be interested in change are either The Questioners or The Learners, as these two groups are the most eager to talk about change (though again, they don't often implement it). The minority are The Maybe or The Absolute teachers. This means that only a small amount within the minority are even in the market for making any type of changes.

Here's a different perspective. Let's say I am speaking to an audience of 500 attentive teachers. Somewhere around 450 of them might be thinking, "This won't work in my classroom" or they will be making note of what words they can say to demonstrate their learning of my content. The remaining 50 might consider using the strategies I am sharing back in their classrooms. Of those 50, maybe 25 will implement the new ideas in order to make a sustained change to their day-to-day instruction. That's a tough audience.

Here's the problem I have with those numbers. I have spent years looking at educational research to determine what every teacher could do every day in his or her classroom to create an efficient and active learning environment. These simple strategies make up my own professional teaching standard and The McCammon Method. Because I believe that most teachers in the United States could follow this standard, I am not satisfied with only reaching 25 out of every 500.

In an attempt to increase my impact, I use a number of strategies to not only reach more of The Maybe or The Absolute teachers, but the strategies can also be used to inspire The Questioner and The Learner because that's the real bread and butter. It's important to start chipping away at the majority and the strategies discussed next have allowed me to inspire all types of teachers to change their day-to-day instruction.

Thousands of teachers are already using one-take lecture videos to solve the problem of time. Thousands of teachers are using the one-take paperslide video strategy to challenge students to create their own content. Thousands of teachers are using my content songs to increase student motivation for learning. Thousands of teachers get students up and moving every day to activate the brain. The coolest thing about my professional teaching standard and my work is that it's all about creating transparent teaching and learning environments. I get to see the video products that teachers and students create in and for the classroom every day.

I realize what I've asked of teachers, and will continue to ask of them, can be a lot; having even the little bit of impact that I've had, getting teachers to change, has been tough. Here are some simple strategies that I've picked up along the way and used to inspire this level of change.

SUGGEST CHANGE

Words matter when introducing new ideas. Instead of commanding change, which is the tool of many policymakers, we can suggest change. It may seem too simple to make a difference, but the devil is in the details. Let me explain.

How and when to suggest change was the most important life lesson I learned from 10 weeks of swing dance classes. When someone like me (a novice dancer) would be dancing socially with an expert, occasionally that expert would feel compelled to tell me something I should or should not be doing. As soon as the words "you should" came out of their mouth, I immediately felt a rush of failure and inadequacy. These feelings made it difficult to process new information or even be open to anything that they were saying. The expert was telling me what to do to improve but my pesky reactance[55] got in the way. They were taking away my options as a dancer, telling me to stop doing the moves I was comfortable with and to try something else.

We were discussing this phenomenon during one of our lessons, and my instructor pointed out that a simple question can make all the difference. "May I make a suggestion?" When asked that question, it allows for two important things to happen. First, it lets me determine whether I am open for a suggestion (criticism) at that exact moment. I can always say, "No, thanks." Second, it gives my brain time to adjust and prepare for a

---

55 Wikipedia: Reactance is a motivational reaction to offers, persons, rules, or regulations that threaten or eliminate specific behavioral freedoms. Reactance occurs when a person feels that someone or something is taking away their choices or limiting the range of alternatives.

suggestion. When I have a moment to prepare an answer to this question, I am more open to the new information because I am given a chance to tell myself, "It's only a suggestion."

Incidentally, many parents use a version of this. Instead of saying, "You have to stop eating bologna and eat your green vegetables," which would cause kids to freak out, many parents will instead say, "Would you like to have spinach or peas with your bologna?" This question allows children to feel like they had a choice in the matter. It is much easier to get kids to eat their vegetables if you give them a choice.

This makes the world of difference when attempting to inspire change in others. Of course, this does not only apply to the world of dance and vegetables. Many of us are in a position to offer suggestions (criticism) to others every day.

So, may I make a suggestion? Use this question often. I ask it many times during my keynotes, workshops and presentations. Yes, sometimes people will say no. It means they are not ready to hear about an alternative to what they are currently doing (and if they say, "Uh, yeah, I guess," that also means no). However, many times, people will say yes. Once I hear "yes," I know they will be better prepared to hear what I have to say and will be more likely to make changes to their practice.

MODEL CHANGE

Every time I am delivering a presentation, I am teaching. I want to model efficient and active learning environments, so that I can engage my students (the participants) in the content I am delivering. Good teaching is not just something I do in typical classrooms. Good teaching is something that I strive to do when presenting to any human audience (I have yet to present to an alien one, but I think I'd still use modeling).

I model the use of video lectures during all my professional development sessions. I make those videos (and all my other video content) available to my students as self-paced resources, so they can revisit my message anywhere and anytime. This is important because it provides immediate support for any teacher who said "yes" when I asked to make a suggestion. If those teachers are inspired to make a change, I'm just a click away to help them with a step-by-step procedure for doing so. If teachers said nothing or "no" when I asked to make a suggestion, then I will still be a click away if they change their mind. It might take years for a teacher to decide they want to change. My YouTube videos will always be freely available and ready for them.

Because I suggest that teachers constantly challenge students to re-teach and record the content, putting it into their own words, I model this teaching method in every presentation by challenging the audience to re-teach my lessons. It only takes a few minutes, and it's the best way for me to know if my participants learned what I wanted them to learn. I put them in groups and have them collaborate to re-teach the lessons. While the groups are discussing, I can walk around the room and listen to the conversations, identifying a participant or two who I want to present their unique lesson to the group. I regularly record their lessons and share them after the session is over.

Finally, I believe students should never sit for long periods of time, so I build movement into my presentations. Students need to be up and moving in every class period. I take pride in being able to get learners up and moving throughout every keynote, presentation and workshop that I facilitate. I have students discuss and kinesthetically demonstrate content, design movements for curriculum-based songs, or just take a walk while answering questions. These simple strategies ignite the brain and create a healthy and active learning environment.

Modeling allows me to show off my skills to teachers who don't usually get to see peers teach. In fact, teachers who attend an event where I am speaking get to experience an innovative teaching method that they likely have never seen before. This, along with constantly using the language of suggestion, allows me to create the best possible environment for inspiring teachers to make changes to their practice.

Modeling has inspired a number of The Questioners and The Learners to change, many of which contacted me years later to tell me that they were convinced that they were doing everything right until they saw me teach. Many tell me that experiencing my teaching was the spark that convinced them to adopt my professional standard in their classroom.

Selling 21ˢᵀ Century Reflection

The third strategy for inspiring change is derived from early education philosophers like Dewey and Schon. They taught us that reflecting on our work is the quickest and most powerful method to practice and improve skills. However, this involves a "willingness to endure a condition of mental unrest and disturbance." This disturbance is often referred to as cognitive dissonance, but I like to call it disequilibrium, which is an economic term meaning a state of being unbalanced.[56]

Each time an educator records him or herself teaching and then watches it back, they will experience disequilibrium. Watching their videos will give them the privilege of looking at themselves honestly, but will make them feel unbalanced, with many saying, "What I thought about myself is quite different from the truth on video." Nothing is more powerful than someone deciding that they need to make a change. Reflective practice is the best way to get a teacher to that point. Nobody can tell a superhero they need to change, except the superhero.

If you have convinced yourself that you are the best teacher possible, this form of reflective practice will help bring you back to reality. It's what

---

56 Reflective Practice. Retrieved from http://schooled.lodgemccammon.com

I experienced when I was forced to watch myself teach that 45-minute lesson during my student teaching. It's also what I experienced years later when I recorded my first one-take video lecture in that conference room at the FI. It was what I experienced when I watched my performance in the TEDx video. I didn't realize it at the time, but I was using the most powerful strategy for both knowing myself honestly and improving my skills. More to the point, I needed to be realistic about my practice if I was going to be open-minded about changing it, and that's exactly what reflective practice allowed me to do.

It was only after I started using video-based reflective practice that my mind truly became open to new ideas. Before reflective practice, I was caught up in trying to hide my insecurities by telling everyone that I was a great teacher. After I looked at myself honestly, and started working toward reaching my true potential (by recording and reflecting on thousands of videos), I am no longer insecure about who I am and what I can do. I have evidence of my skills and I am realistic about my abilities because I am able to compare my videos to the videos of other expert teachers on YouTube. Reflective practice allows me to be honest about my growth as a teacher, speaker, musician and dancer by looking back on videos from years ago and compare them to videos I created yesterday. This is an extremely low-barrier strategy for improvement that every teacher can work toward, simply by taking their phone out of their pocket and hitting record.

We Did It!

You just read "Schooled: The Story of an Education." Was it the worst book about education ever written? Was it the best? Was it somewhere in between? In any case, may I make one last suggestion? (If yes, keep reading)

Think back through the lessons you learned over the past 100+ pages and record a concise one-take video using your cell phone that teaches the book back to me. Review and reflect on that video. Send me that video (I could use the feedback). Then use the same process to document all the lessons in your life.[57]

---

57 Don't Wait for Permission to Share Your Ideas. Retrieved from http://schooled.lodgemccammon.com

AUTHOR BIOGRAPHY

• • •

Dr. Lodge McCammon holds a PhD in curriculum development from North Carolina State University, and he has taught civics and economics at the high school level. He now works as an international education consultant and offers keynote speeches, workshops, curriculum development, and a variety of training programs. His passion is to help fellow educators implement innovative classroom strategies that get students more engaged in learning. To learn more, visit his YouTube channel or website, www.lodgemccammon.com.

Made in the USA
Middletown, DE
21 July 2020